T0268045

11 Lives

11

Lives

Stories from Palestinian Exile

Nadia Fahed | Intisar Hajaj | Yafa Talal El-Masri
Youssef Naanaa | Ruba Rahme | Hanin Mohammad Rashid
Mira Sidawi | Wedad Taha | Salem Yassin
Taha Younis | Mahmoud Mohammad Zeidan

Edited and Translated by
Muhammad Ali Khalidi

with an Introduction by
Perla Issa

OR Books
New York · London

مؤسسة الدراسات الفلسطينية
Institute for Palestine Studies

Co-published with the Institute for Palestine Studies

© 2022 Muhammad Ali Khalidi

Published by OR Books, New York and London

Visit our website at www.orbooks.com

All rights information: rights@orbooks.com

First printing 2022

Cataloging-in-Publication data is available from the Library of Congress.
A catalog record for this book is available from the British Library.

Typeset by Lapiz Digital Services.

paperback ISBN 978-1-68219-347-1 • ebook ISBN 978-1-68219-348-8

Contents

Translator's Note and Acknowledgments

This collection of autobiographical essays by eleven Palestinian refugees about their lives, loves, yearnings, and losses, is a unique document, since it constitutes a rare opportunity for refugees themselves to narrate the twists and turns in their own lives. Though none of them were trained as writers, each of these authors has a distinctive voice and approach, some confessional, others formal, some narrative, others impressionistic, all drawing attention to different facets of life in exile for Palestinians. As translator, I feel privileged to have been able to convey their hopes and dreams—as well as their fears and nightmares—and have tried as far as possible to adhere to the literal meanings of their words, while attempting to convey something of their varying tones and moods.

The creative writing workshop that this book is based on was the brainchild of Perla Issa, researcher and senior fellow at the Institute for Palestine Studies (IPS). In 2018, she had the idea of advertising a workshop in autobiographical writing to the community of Palestinian refugees in Lebanon. As a result of that open call, eleven people were chosen to participate in the twelve sessions of the workshop. They gathered each week in Beirut under the capable guidance of Lebanese novelist Hassan Daoud to share their manuscripts and try out their ideas. The result would not have been as honed, crafted, and polished without Daoud's literary skill and expertise. I have tried to intrude as little as possible on the authors' own words, but have occasionally added a word or phrase in parentheses to clarify the meaning. Proper names and Arabic words that may not be familiar to some readers have been defined in a Glossary at the end of the book.

This translation owes its existence to a number of people at OR Books and IPS. At OR Books, Catherine Cumming expertly edited my translations from the Arabic, which were often literal to the point of clumsiness, rearranging sentences and reanimating paragraphs, with the aim of better conveying the authors' prose in idiomatic English. She was also supremely patient during the production stages, overseeing the cover and overall design of the book, among many other things. Many thanks are also due to Colin Robinson, who saw the value in the project from the beginning and supported it to the end. At IPS, in addition to the indispensable role of Perla Issa, each in their own ways, Stephen Bennett, Khalid Farraj, and Rashid Khalidi all played a part in seeing the book to fruition. But my greatest thanks goes to the authors themselves, who entrusted their stories to me, in the hope that I have reflected them faithfully, and have borne witness to their collective love for Palestine.

M. A. K.
New York, 2022

Introduction

Writing Palestinian Exile through
Autobiographical Essays

The history of the Palestinian people has been one of constant war, occupation, and exile. Since the 1948 Nakba, the
Palestinian experience has been one of continuous fragmentation and dispersal. These multiple displacements engen-
dered myriad trajectories for the individual refugee. Starting
from their initial exodus from Palestine in 1948, the fate
of Palestinian refugees has depended on numerous factors
such as which country they sought refuge in, what sect they
belonged to, what wars visited them, and what laws they
were subjected to. Just as snowflakes, which originate in the
same cloud, gain unique shapes and sizes as they tumble
through the air, swirling and spiraling, so do Palestinians
take on unique journeys as they face various political, legal,
and economic realities. In that sense each Palestinian story
is unique, and each story tells the story of all Palestinians.

I know this firsthand, though it took me twenty-three
years to start learning my own story. Born in Lebanon during the civil war, I only discovered my Palestinian roots
rather late in life. I was born with a Lebanese citizenship
and was not subjected to the systematic discrimination and
economic marginalization that Palestinian refugees face in
Lebanon. For many years I thought that my personal story
did not qualify as a "Palestinian story" as it did not bear

the signs of physical and economic violence that are the emblem of Palestinian life in Lebanon. In a sense I felt that I did not deserve to be called Palestinian. It took me time to accept that while my story may be different, it is no less a Palestinian story, and its meaning can only be revealed when put next to other Palestinian tales.

This is the idea behind the book you are reading today. It is a collection of short essays written by Palestinian refugees in Lebanon about their personal experiences in life. It is the outcome of a creative writing workshop entitled Writing the Palestinian Exile Through Autobiographical Essays that was held at the Institute for Palestine Studies in the winter of 2016/2017, and was supported by Selat: Links through the Arts, a project launched by A. M. Qattan Foundation (Palestine) in partnership with Prince Claus Fund (Netherlands).

Eleven participants were chosen from an open call to participate in a creative writing workshop led by the renowned Lebanese writer Hassan Daoud. Participants were predominantly women and their ages ranged from the twenties to the fifties. This was not by design but was the organic outcome of the open call. The workshop, consisting of twelve sessions, aimed to coach Palestinian refugees from Lebanon to write autobiographical essays in Arabic, with an end goal of producing the edited book you are currently holding: a collection of stories about Palestinian refugees written by the protagonists themselves.

The other reason for holding the workshop was a desire to engage with the Palestinian community in Lebanon in a different way than as objects of research. As an academic institution, we at the Institute for Palestine Studies often conduct and publish studies that speak in the name of Palestinian refugees, describing their lives and recounting their stories. With the workshop, we wanted to give a chance to the refugees to write about their own lives and gain credit for it through the publication of the book. We wanted to relate to the Palestinian community in Lebanon not as objects of study but as subjects able to narrate their own tales in their own words. However, once the workshop began, I realized that it was not that simple and that my intentions may not have been so pristine. Participants often challenged the purpose of the workshop: the writing of autobiographical texts. They would ask me: What do you mean by autobiographical essays? Can't we write about others? About a neighbor, about a friend? Some did not want to write about themselves. Some wanted to include fiction in their stories. These repeated questions made me realize that by defining the goal of the workshop as the writing of autobiographical essays, I was again acting like the researcher who descends upon the community imposing their own agenda with a desire to extract particular information about people's lives. In my initial vision for the project, I saw this as an opportunity for readers to access the "true story" of the refugees, unfiltered by others, whether they be academics, journalists, or literary authors. I wanted access to the private, the unseen, the personal; the details that only those who live the life would know. Just as in my academic studies, I was again driven by a desire to uncover the hidden, to gain more information about the lives of Palestinian refugees, as if that were a goal whose importance is unquestionable. With time, and as these discussions persisted, I relented. I realized my own narrow-mindedness and accepted that participants write about what they deemed fit. But in the end, it seems that most participants incorporated my initial desire to write autobiographical essays and that is what they produced.

In this book, you will find a wide variety of essays, each recounting a different life, a different tale, a different opinion, each particular to its author. Some wrote about life in the refugee camps but using vastly different angles. Salem Yassin artfully describes his coming-of-age experiences in a refugee camp through what he calls "the people's free newspaper": the graffiti on walls. Mira Sidawi blurs the line between fantasy and reality to turn the ordinary into extraordinary. Taha Younis moves skillfully between the present and the past, between childhood and adulthood, recounting with chilling honesty his personal experiences, while Nadia Fahed describes with humor and simplicity the daily challenges she faced taking care of her young daughter as well as her aging grandmother. Finally, Youssef Naanaa brings life and laughter to the small Palestinian gathering Da'uq through the daily activities of his extended family. Other participants preferred to use this opportunity to reflect. Yafa Talal El-Masri ponders the meaning of exile through a discussion of her dreams, friendships, and family relations, while Hanin Mohammad Rashid reflects upon the meaning of her name in relation to her father's and grandmother's lives. In contrast, Wedad Taha draws on her life from early childhood in the Emirates to adulthood in Lebanon, where she came face to face with a Palestinian society she disavows. Some preferred to write about the Nakba. Intisar Hajaj recounts the quintessential Palestinian experience through the story of her maternal grandmother, Khadijeh, a Lebanese woman who lived a Palestinian life, while Ruba Rahme moves us back to the painful present, to the latest Nakba: the flight and dispersal of the Palestinian refugees from Syria. Finally, in an essay that resembles more an eyewitness account than a literary text, Mahmoud Mohammad Zeidan documents in painstaking detail the occupation of 'Ayn al-Hilweh camp by Israeli forces in 1982, as he lived it when he was just thirteen years old. In the end, what joins these essays together is their deeply personal nature; they reveal the lives and thoughts of ordinary people whose voices we seldom hear.

There is no need to say more, the texts say it all.

Graffiti from a Time Gone By

SALEM YASSIN

(b. Miyeh wa Miyeh refugee camp, Saida, Lebanon, 1966)

This is where I grew up: in a Palestinian refugee camp among eleven brothers and sisters, and the sun and the moon, in a home with three rooms and a tin-covered roof. That roof was the reason I hid behind a voice that could barely be heard, a voice that nearly disappeared in winter. The sound of the rain colliding against that roof, and the hubbub of raucous voices, drowned out soft voices such as mine and prevented them from reaching their destinations.

I was born nine years before the outbreak of the Lebanese civil war, in which Palestinians played a principal role as both fuel and fire. I lived through the war's blaze as a hostage of the camp, confined between the house of Umm Anwar and the empty lot of Abu Na'meh.

Pictures of martyrs climbed the walls of our home, their eyes peering out at passersby, calling them by their names and nicknames, telegraphing to them the injustice of their deaths. The revolutionary songs playing over the loudspeakers echoed throughout the camp, blending together in my memory with the hum of the 'Ain al-Rummaneh bus.

My childhood dreams sprouted in the alleyways of the camp and blossomed among dreary stone walls, in a humid atmosphere that weighed upon the heart.

It was there that I experienced days of war, death, and sadness, as well as of peace and love. There, I had my first kiss, and sang dolefully with Shaykh Imam during long evening vigils, drinking tea under the mulberry tree: "My love of words conquers my silence, and my hatred of silence brings me woe."

As a boy, before I knew my left from my right, I learned to navigate the byways of the camp by following the exposed water channels. I could go anywhere by tracing the open sewers carrying putrid water through the winding alleyways. I struggled along the narrow paths and sidled up to the carriage that delivered flour rations, tussling with the driver every time and coming home coated in flour. My grandmother Sa'da would laugh and say: "You poor white thing, you look like a flea who fell into the yogurt!"

I learned to read and write in the UNRWA schools, which freshened my awareness of the writing that adorned the cold walls of the camp. The words were no longer talismans stuck on the walls from time immemorial; I could now recognize new, brighter inscriptions appearing daily. These were the headlines of the people's free newspaper. Each time we lived through an event, someone would issue a silent scream on one of the walls, in a spontaneous burst of words that might be misspelled or grammatically incorrect, but nevertheless gave the wall added value and color. The words, mainly written in secret, attracted the attention of all the people of the camp. They became stored in the memory of the alleyways and incorporated into our sense of place and space.

Soft voices could become strident like the call to prayer when expressed on the walls of tin-covered houses. These inscriptions, whose signatories are anonymous, were honest and unambiguous, unlike the official newspaper, whose skimpy reports were disingenuous and subject to censorship by the security services.

The walls of the camp, erected to house refugees in a civilized and refined manner, were transformed by words into mirrors of our lives and of current events. They conveyed a message that set them apart from all other walls in the world.

These walls lived and breathed, were born and died, had nicknames, and grew haphazardly like wild berry bushes in dimensions that defied the norms of architecture. Barred from expanding horizontally, our walls grew vertically from earth to sky, against the direction of the lord's merciful rain. And, in times of war, they grew deep underground to create a martyr's grave or a child's bomb shelter.

The walls of the camp carried death sentences and marked the confines of a prison whose strict limits were set by a rental lease. The landlords didn't seem to realize, with the feigned innocence of hospitality and humanitarianism, that people tend to multiply after a hundred years of solitude—or rather, after ninety-nine years. The leases on our homes were set to expire at ninety-nine years to ensure that they would never become our property, according to the idiotic law of a nation that sees its future in past glories.

The stray words that here and there decorated the walls were penned, deliberately and with intent, by men who disappeared into the pages of an extemporaneous history. The words carved grooves into the memory, spinning stories that were never spoken but were seen in faded colors, leaning lazily, layered on the walls of the camp's houses, by anyone who could decipher them.

Each sentence engraved by a man's hand amounted to a "Communique No. 1," or a draft will and testament for a martyr. Many of their words spoke for themselves, while the meanings of others remained in the depths of the sea. Palestine, our "dead sea" that rages and swells forever,

"We will come to you, my homeland, when the winds of our love carry us back over land and sea."

The words hung like icons on the walls of the alleyways where strangers always got lost, getting dizzy wandering in circles.

"Oh, wise wanderer, your only guide is the speech of the eyes."

These mute walls preserve all our secrets, starting with the whispers of love that compose our very lives and ending with our silent deaths.

"Palestine, eternal wound of time!"

"I love you," with a picture of a bleeding heart.

A colorless rose with the first initials of two lovers.

A map of the lost homeland.

"Pevolution until victory," scrawled with the messy tar used to pave the main street of the camp.

Thick straight lines smudged with handprints, remaining visible on the wall of Abu Salma's house despite being covered in layers of whitewash mixed with yellow ocher.

Words etched by the "school dunce" on the walls of the camp school, marking his presence years after his body disappeared in a martyrdom operation "on the inside." I remember walking in his funeral procession, wondering about the contents of the coffin the men carried on their shoulders. It was shrouded in the flag of Palestine, wreathed with roses, and draped with a sash commemorating the martyr in the name of the revolution.

"The coffin contains pieces of his body."

"The coffin contains his revolutionary uniform, his mother's shawl, and his father's prayer beads."

"No, the coffin's empty!"

That's what the women whispered, shielding their mouths with the fringes of their shawls, while walking along on the periphery of the funeral procession.

"Symbolic funeral" was the hushed expression that my ears picked out from the murmurings of the assembled crowd. From that day, the "symbolic" lodged itself in my personal dictionary in association with images of funerals and martyrs.

The story of the "dunce" is just one of many that sits alongside those of Abu Jildeh, who tortured dogs with his whip, Nu'man the feverish lover, Arnoub the fan of the Shu'lah football team, and other anonymous teachers whose lessons are taught in deafening silence on the walls of the camp school.

As I grew, I became aware not only of the writing on the walls, but of the large banners that sagged under the weight of all the words emblazoned on them, and the smaller ones with short dense words, like the one hanging near the Abu Lubnan coffee shop, which read: "Keep Your Hands Off Vietnam!" Because it defied our comprehension, my friends and I assumed that it was the work of the Popular Front, which we avoided getting close to because of its "complexities." Once, though, the leader of our gang, 'Arif—who was a couple of years older than the rest of us, more impressive looking, and more mischievous—decided that we should leave Fateh because he was "unconvinced" by the party, and that we should instead "enlist" in the Popular Front. We couldn't oppose his decision. We went straight to the Popular Front and piled into the makeshift office like the stray cats that crowded the butcher shop of Abu Mamduh. The cups of tea were the same as in the offices of Fateh: sweet and dark, poured from a charred kettle. But here everyone read and smoked. The adjoining room contained stacks of books with thick red covers in an incomprehensible language. 'Arif alerted me to this treasure with a wink, which I immediately understood. The latest trend in the camp was to make little red vases out of these books (propaganda from foreign governments) distributed by the Popular Front. So we took more than our fair share, using them for crafting and bestowing some of them on the youngsters who begged us: "For the love of God! For the sake of your mother! On your sister's honor! Please give me a red book!" We'd save our most charitable act, however, for the most groveling beggars; namely the gift of the large book with the dark blue cover. So it was all because we "loved God and cherished our mothers and sisters" that we sacrificed our opportunity to don a uniform and carry a torch in that year's annual march celebrating the founding of Fateh.

It was not long before 'Arif got tired of the red vases and announced that we should return to Fateh. It's true that the Fateh logo was harder to draw on the wall than that of the Popular Front. But it also depicted two machine guns and a grenade, which was more powerful than the Popular Front arrow. Plus, according to 'Arif, Fateh was much larger than the Popular Front, which "only had seven hundred

and seven cadres." This was how his little brain had interpreted the number that we always drew alongside the logo.
No one had explained to us that it symbolized the hijack-
ing of a Boeing 707 aircraft by the Popular Front in 1970.
So we all returned to Fateh—all but Ahmad al-'Affar, who
declared that al-Sa'iqa (the Lightning Bolt) was stronger
than al-'Asifa (the Storm). We started to spy on him from
afar, watching as he and others lit fires from straw in the
low-lying areas at the far end of the Jalloul neighborhood,
leaping over the flames. We never dared join their organization, but we were forced to increase our drawings of our
own slogans on the walls once we started seeing the slogan
"Men of Fire" appear in charcoal on the yellow walls of
the UNRWA bathrooms and the garbage incinerator. We all
ignored, however, a lone slogan written in a distinctive font
that read: "Jund Allah (Soldiers of God)." We didn't have
the energy to grapple with whoever this villain was who
had introduced God and his soldiers into our battle! We
were not capable of engaging in a war of attrition that would
inevitably end in our defeat.

I wasn't always convinced by 'Arif, whose face as an
infant had been washed with his own urine by the midwife
Salma "to make him shameless." He was a true mastermind
who made sure that he had a finger in every pie. I continued
to search for the real reason that drove 'Arif to return us
to Fateh, until one evening he revealed all to me: he had
heard from his father that Fateh would soon be distributing
"meat—sheep with tails—an overflowing storehouse full."
Then 'Arif revealed to me his parting shot. Before leaving
the Popular Front, he had torn from each red book the thin
parchment paper that covered the image of "Kim Sung,"

which came right after the cover page, and he was going to use this as tracing paper to copy the Fateh logo!

Words leap from the walls and resonate in my mind, evoking the memories I folded into the alleys of the camp. Once, I was forced to take a break from our wheelings and dealings as a result of being stricken with jaundice. I had pains in my lower chest and my eyes turned "as yellow as the pastries on the bakery cart," as my mother put it, God rest her soul. But illness and isolation did not make me sad, since the jar of honey that was reserved for me and me alone was enough to gladden my heart. I exaggerated my pained gestures for the benefit of my guests, never forgetting to clutch at my lower chest, so as to justify my exclusive right to the honey just in case one of my siblings had the inclination to taste it.

One day I was visited by my most precious childhood friend, gentle Khalil. I regaled him with the tale of how I discovered that I was ill when I noticed that my urine had changed color to a brownish red, and how I alerted my father who immediately took me to the doctor. But before I had the opportunity to sing the doctor's praises and boast about the honey that I had enjoyed in my isolation, Khalil suddenly interrupted me, with a tear glinting in his eye: "If I were you, I wouldn't have told anyone about it. I would just have written on the walls: Down with the isolationist forces!"

We soon resumed our usual internecine wars. No disease could deter us from our buffoonish duties. Our gang's exploits were seasonally based and consisted of raiding the fields of fava beans, chickpeas, and watermelons, and the orchards of almonds and oranges, that lay close to the camp. The loveliest seasons were those of grapes and figs, since the trees were plentiful and easy to reach. But we didn't restrict ourselves to raiding fruits; we also caught small birds in their nests. We could distinguish types of birds from their nests—the materials used, the construction, the color of the eggs—and from the different kinds of trees they built them in. Our usual habit was to walk around and scope the trees, noting the locations of the nests and committing them to memory. We would then monitor the progress of the hatchlings until they were mature enough for us to catch and raise at home. We fed them by dripping liquid into their tiny beaks from the thin end of a stick.

The cleverest kid in our cohort when it came to these matters was Salman Ghazi, who stalked the trees alone without letting anyone in on the action. One day, myself and some other members of our gang were out in one of the fields where Salman roamed, when I noticed that several of the trees in which we had located nests had mud on their trunks. It looked as though someone had left footprints after climbing up. When I investigated further, I noticed that symbols had been scratched into the bark of each of the trees. I tried to detect a connection between them and the letters of Salman's name or nickname but couldn't, and it suddenly dawned on me that they designated the type of bird nesting in each tree. We went on to conduct a wide-ranging tour of the area in the full flush of victory, since we now had the locations of all of Salman's nests without any effort on our part. We didn't have to clamber up the trunks to search through the dense branches of the trees, or crane our necks to peer into their upper reaches. We could just glance at each trunk to know what kind of treasure awaited us up above. The race was on: we just had to wait for the eggs to hatch and for the first fluff of feathers to form on the hatchlings. Then we could capture them before they could fly. As for Salman, we could just tell him: "The early bird catches the worm."

One day we all met in the Tabrani cave in Abu Ni'meh to roast some "hazelnuts" in season. These were actually seeds gathered from sorrel plants by moles and stored underground, which sprouted in abundance in the winter. We would find the "hazelnut storehouse" and collect the seeds to then roast in a tin can from a nearby junkyard. We were all gathered around the fire when suddenly 'Arif extracted from his shirtsleeve some cigarettes and shoved one in my direction, saying: "Smoke!" It was an unfiltered Lucky Strike. "Or would you rather have a sissy Kent cigarette after your illness?"

That was a dramatic and magical leap on 'Arif's part. We were used to smoking the dried leaves of grapevines and fig trees, which we crumbled and rolled up in newspaper to smoke. For an added fancy flavor we would mix in some dried mint. If 'Arif wanted to show off, he would stuff his "pipe" with a mix of dried leaves. The pipe was made from the coarse husk of an acorn, in which a hole was drilled to insert a straw. He would light the pipe and stretch out his long legs, like those of a praying mantis, before taking a deep drag while closing one of his eyes and raising the other eyebrow. We would laugh and call him "Barbar Agha," after the fabled Ottoman ruler. But for 'Arif to bring real tobacco was serious stuff, and without a doubt the sign of a real man. I took the cigarette and smoked it silently, trying not to choke on my suppressed coughs.

Suddenly, a sound like thunder assaulted us and shook the ground underneath. It was Abu 'Aziz Ayub, who was out hunting with his dog Golda. Abu 'Aziz was a respected and fearsome military commander in the Palestinian revolution, and he was distantly related to 'Arif on his mother's side. He rained down blows on us like a beast. Not a single one of us escaped a slap or a punch before we all ran off with our feet higher than our heads, leaving 'Arif behind to face his fate and the wrath of his mother, Na'mat. Some of the women secretly called her Naqmat (Retribution). She was a formidable widow who would fill her mouth with kerosene, light a match, and spray the liquid from her lips to target the flies swarming around the mulberries that fell onto her courtyard. In a split second they would be incinerated, their wings and legs burnt off, their bodies spinning on the ground. Then she would let her hens and chicks loose to feed on them.

One day we awoke to the sound of screaming and cursing. It was Abu 'Aziz Ayub, fuming with rage and vowing to kill all the inhabitants of the camp ("those sons of bitches!"). Someone had climbed over the wall around his house and wreaked havoc in his garden, pouring tar all over the trees, plants, and walls. Worst of all: they had also hanged Golda on a tree branch. Abu 'Aziz's garden was a splendid plot that had started out as a small onion patch and expanded by dint of a policy of annexation and appropriation. He would erect tin roofing panels around the perimeter and then move them, pushing them forward bit by bit, to enlarge his garden, and no one dared to stop him. As for us, we never had the nerve to think about approaching the garden or defiling its tempting white wall with even a single mark, lest we provoke the wrath of the beast and his dog. Unidentified perpetrator, how formidable you were!

Though in truth, we never had any doubt as to the identity of the perpetrator. After careful investigation, we noticed a word daubed in tar in the corner of Abu 'Aziz's wall in a hand that we knew well. 'Arif had slanted his writing slightly to the right and appeared to have used his left hand in an attempt at disguise. It read: "Traitor."

'Arif had changed. As well as the smoking, he had carved real tattoos into his biceps: the word "Palestine" and an image of a scorpion. It was as though the walls of the camp could no longer hold his words and so he had begun to engrave them on his body. His arms became a moving banner displaying eternal words.

We no longer dared approach 'Arif the Scorpion, though we occasionally saw him in his narrow jeans with a box of Marlboros displayed prominently in the pocket of his see-through shirt. We gathered anecdotes about his militant activities with his new gang, such as filling empty bullet-casings with the yellow gunpowder used in hunting rifles and detonating them in the valley. His technique consisted of sealing the refilled bullet-casing with a stone, leaving a small opening for the insertion of a fuse made of gunpowder twisted up in fine paper. He would light the fuse and then run to the shelter of a nearby tree. A few seconds later, his bomb would explode and 'Arif would emerge to survey the damage. He would let out a long laugh whose pitch was proportional to his degree of satisfaction with the results.

We got used to the sound of 'Arif's explosions and the Armed Struggle security forces got used to arresting him without even asking him whether he was responsible or not. One of 'Arif's most fabled exploits took place after he got fed up with the security forces and was driven to hatch a diabolical plot. He went down to the valley, having prepared a hefty explosive charge made up of casings from a 14.5-caliber anti-aircraft gun, which were attached by a short fuse to a mosquito-repellent incense coil. After lighting the slow-burning coil, he scrambled up the valley to the security forces' office. "Hey guys! Do you mind sharing a cup of tea?" On the first sip of the third cup of tea, the huge explosion went off. "It's not me! It's not me!" he sputtered, as he sprayed everyone with tea, "You see: God has revealed the truth."

Once, around sunset, I came face to face with the "Scorpion" near the entrance to the alleyway leading to our house. He blocked my way with his ample stature and laughed as he slapped my neck, saying: "There are hazelnuts in Abu 'Aziz Ayub's plot of land."

Around a year later, we learned that the "Scorpion" and his comrades had fallen in combat at the crusader castle at Beaufort, in southern Lebanon, in fierce clashes with Israeli forces. At the funeral, the coffin was draped with banners and the sounds of heavy gunfire and revolutionary ballads rang in the air. But none of it could ease our sadness for the departed leader.

That night we took our spray cans and spread out across the camp. We covered all available and unavailable space, painting over all the old dusty slogans: "Forces of the Heroic Martyr 'Arif the Scorpion." It was our way of honoring the martyr whose "blood flowed on the battlefield so as to make it bloom every spring with red anemones," as the PLO eulogy stated. On the walls of the martyr's house, I drew a scorpion to the best of my artistic abilities, under which I wrote: "If time passes and you don't see me, this is my portrait by which to remember me." I signed it with his initials: "A. S."

One day, not long afterward, I sat in the shade of an olive tree, smoking and scratching at the soil with a piece of wood. I was filled with a sense of cosmic boredom and felt a quiet rage overcoming me. It swelled in my chest and crashed against my sides, spraying me with questions that settled in my numb brain without receiving any answers. I picked up a rusty nail and began to score the bark of the branch hanging nearest me. I etched it with the first words that came to mind: "Palestine is a bride and its dowry is blood."

Suddenly, I heard the voice of Nazmi al-Tahir behind me: "Do you want me to tattoo it on you?" He added, "My fee is a box of tobacco." Without hesitation, I stretched out my arm, saying: "I have ten cigarettes, but I want you to write something else: 'Until when,' followed by a large question mark."

After weighing my offer against the amount of effort required and the surface area of my scrawny biceps, he agreed, albeit shaking his head in bewilderment at the phrase I had selected: "I can't make head or tail of it." It was completely alien to his store of practiced phrases, but "the customer is always right." He reached into his pocket and took out the equipment for this baptism of masculinity. It consisted of a sewing needle, ink pen, rubber band, and lighter. He traced out the tattoo on my arm with the pen, then he broke the pen and emptied the ink out into the cap. After that, he heated the rubber band over the lighter flame, melted it into the ink, and mixed the two ingredients. He sterilized the needle with the flame from the lighter and set to work on my arm, alternately dipping the tip of the needle into the mixture and pricking it into my arm, without diverging from the lines he had drawn. His small blows never faltered and never lost their force or momentum. He only paused to wipe my blood with the tip of a cloth rag. Terrible pain froze the blood in my head and choked up my throat, but crying was out of the question.

The torturous experience ended when he tied the rag around my arm and said: "Leave it covered and don't wash it. The wound will get inflamed a bit, but you'll be fine in a couple of days." Then he added, tapping his fingers against the ten cigarettes in his pocket, "I charged you half-price and am forgiving the rest. It's my donation for the love of God! Congratulations!"

I immediately got up, undid the cloth wrapped around my arm, and wandered the length and breadth of the camp's alleyways. To everything I met—people, stones, the words on the walls, even refuge itself and this entire existence—I brandished my right arm: "Until when?"

Words remain tattooed plainly on arms or walls, between the Nakba and the Naksa, throughout defeats and massacres, love affairs and revolutions, and in a vanquished era when spirits yearn for the right to pledge allegiance in the shadow of a flag. After their migration from people's souls to unlined walls, they persist in feverish exile.

Let us hope that life will be breathed into our words, which reverberate for all time on the walls of refuge and the limbs of our bodies, and that they will be heard openly across all borders. Then the world may come to realize: We write, therefore we exist.

We take such pride in our small cosmic wars. We are the masters of our neighborhoods and alleyways, we are the "free writers," and we alone own the word!

I'm Not Dead Yet

MIRA SIDAWI

(b. Beirut, 1984)

The scenario in my head is very vivid. I stop breathing, it appears as though I'm dead. I'm carried to the cemetery in the Burj al-Barajneh refugee camp and I'm buried. I don't like this scenario. I'd prefer to be buried in a different place. The cemetery in the Burj refugee camp is haunted by the corpses of my father and sister, and I think I'd prefer somewhere more spacious. For me alone. I'd be fine in a green space. Yes, a green space surrounded on all sides by the sea. And before my death I might hang my name on all the trees in that land.

I know, I spout all this rubbish to overcome the inane longing inside of me. What I really want is to be buried in Acre. Why not? I affirm and solemnly swear one hundred times that I will not rise up from the earth to blow myself up, and I will not harm those who colonize the land. I'm a very peaceful individual; I wouldn't harm an ant and I don't swipe at the mosquitoes that fly over my head at night. I'm always focused on my breathing and on practicing calmness, and I'm not bothered at all by the narrow alleyways of the camp or the rats. I adore rats. I don't complain about anything. To me, everything is rosy and joyous. I welcome the rain when it comes down on my head. I celebrate when war breaks out and when someone I love dies in war. It's normal, everything is normal: my blue identity card, my meagre cash, the airplane that takes off and lands again every couple of hours in front of me in the camp. I accept all of this as normal. I have no issues except this burial thing. I need a grave that fits me and nothing else.

Privacy in death is very important; it's virtually the only right that still stands in the event that your other rights are usurped. Frankly—I won't lie—I never understood politics and I can't speak eloquently about a country that I've never lived in. But I feel a strange sensation every time Abu 'Imad, my unemployed friend in the camp, utters the word "Acre." Maybe it's the mysteriousness of its meaning that stirs me. As a refugee, I have the honor of enjoying the special and important privilege of fantasy. Every time Abu 'Imad says "Acre," I get a slight ache in my stomach and become quite incapable of preventing my mind from going to that mysterious place. In fact, I'm quite adept at producing a steady stream of fantasies about things I don't know, God, the mystery of existence, or Acre.

Right away, I imagine myself in a boat no larger than the palm of my hand. Yes, my palm. It is a very small boat that I sleep in under the sun, while Acre shades my body with its hands, and I'm enveloped by a smell that is close to cinnamon. I love cinnamon. And Acre's smell is like cinnamon— or is it rather like fish? Yes, like fish. Anyway, I'm in a boat, giant trees surround me, birds mask the color of the sky, or rather the sky masks the birds. Yes, the sky there is mobile. Everything seems mobile in Acre, apart from me, the only static thing in that place.

Abu 'Imad is not impressed by my constant daydreaming and he always interrupts it with what he calls "a proper cup of tea." I drink tea with him, for no clear reason. Every day, I ask myself why I don't break the habit of drinking tea in the afternoon with this man. Anyway, I give myself over to this custom in front of his house. When he brings the tea, he seems to me like a traditional Englishman putting on a proper tea party. He drinks, converses, analyzes, curses Abu Mazin a hundred times, depending on his mood, and I just listen. As I said before, momentous issues don't concern me at all. But each time I see him, Abu 'Imad becomes more intent on drawing me into the conversation and arousing my enthusiasm for the stories that he tells. He jumps around like a clown in front of me, cursing Oslo, and exclaiming: "It's a piece of paper that I wouldn't use to wipe my ass." My daydreams return. I imagine Abu 'Imad meeting with the leaders of the country, wherever they may be, shining among them, and repeating his famous statement: "I wouldn't even wipe my ass with it." It would be very interesting to observe him confronting President Bush. Bush, with his short hair and large ears, as Abu 'Imad describes him, and he with his scruffy kufiyah and the cigarette that never leaves his lips. Abu 'Imad might discuss with him the whole issue of our country. He might say to the president: "You and your presidency are not more precious than my grandfather's sweetheart, whom he left in Acre at the time of the Nakba."

Abu 'Imad is proud of his grandfather's love story in Acre. Passion before the Nakba, according to Abu 'Imad, is more valuable than passion afterward. When love is mixed with exodus and migration it acquires a sharp taste like ginger. We're not talking about just any exodus and migration, which afflict people generally. We're talking, as he says, about "Palestine."

Abu 'Imad keeps coming back to Palestine. Whether it's his daughter Fatima's divorce, or her children's failure at school, or the United Nations Relief and Works Agency (UNRWA), or the militant factions, Palestine is the large gold stamp that concludes all his stories, ushering in a long silence, before the announcement that the tea party is over.

I remember well how Abu 'Imad died. He got the best death, according to our neighbor Ayyubeh, a retired midwife. I don't deny that I envied him for a long time. "Better than a martyr's death," said Ayyubeh, describing how he shined in the end. The man chose to die free of everything and on his own terms.

Once, a Lebanese friend gifted Abu 'Imad a parrot, and the whole camp went crazy, singing and dancing around the bird. We didn't sleep that night; the whole Tarshiha quarter in the Burj camp was seized by a collective hysteria. Everyone participated in finding a larger cage for the parrot and, unusually, we all reached a consensus about what to feed it. Dr. Fahmi at Haifa Hospital was consulted about the parrot's state of health, and he confirmed that "the parrot is a lion, rivalling Abu Hasan Salameh in his heyday." Everyone took their picture with the parrot, who was considered a new refugee from the parrot species. It was a valuable species, not easily acquired. During the night, everyone gathered outside Abu 'Imad's house and together we settled on nickname for the parrot, calling him "Victory."

Everyone in the neighborhood, whichever faction they belong to, agrees on three watchwords: victory, the right of return, and Abu 'Ammar (Yasir 'Arafat). Of course, they disagree about everything else. Each faction is skilled at blaming another faction whenever someone dies by electrocution, drugs, or just the usual despair.

What matters is that the neighborhood seemed colorful that day, and my personal tea party with Abu 'Imad was transformed into a celebration of the camp's new parrot. Cups of tea were distributed among those present, Abu 'Imad played an Umm Kulthum song, and heads swayed to the rhythm. The celebration was attended by the muezzin of the mosque, Abu Iyad, who enjoyed the voice of the diva. He waited for his turn to recite the sura of Yasin (from the Qur'an) to bless the parrot and protect it from the evil eye.

To my eye, everything was wonderful. For a moment, the camp seemed spacious, wider than the boat in the sea off the coast of Acre. I wished I could write the following message on the wall where the posters of the leaders hung: "The camp is also a boat, but one without a sea. We are the sea." I waxed poetic in the face of all the joy that overcame the children, the walls, the cats, and even the rats.

On the third day that the parrot resided with Abu 'Imad, the man woke up to the reality that his bird had died. He tried repeatedly to revive him and to speak to his stiff body, but it didn't change anything. Everyone grieved the parrot's death, and some said sarcastically that it couldn't acclimate inside the camp; it was simply not a refugee. It was a child of privilege with an illustrious pedigree.

After that, I saw before me a different Abu 'Imad. He'd told me one day, before the parrot was buried in the camp's cemetery, that death either brings on laughter or it strikes you like a dagger and disappears. That's what that parrot did to Abu 'Imad. The regular afternoon tea parties came to an end. He withdrew into isolation, closing his door behind him, leaving his birdcage empty.

Some time later, I saw Abu 'Imad's door open again to let in the light, and he emerged elegant, wearing a simple, hopeful expression. And he never came back. It was said in the report of his death that he was standing around with some of the young men in Mar Elias camp—specifically in front of the office of the Bureau of Refugee Affairs—and that one of the men told a joke and Abu 'Imad couldn't control himself, so he laughed and chuckled until he died.

When I was little, my aunt would take me by the hand and lead me around the whole camp. Between incantations, she would insist that we would find the welfare office open. At that time, the only thing that concerned me was the kite I saw on television circling the skies of the city. For a long time, I dreamt of a kite like that. I imagined myself holding on to the strings of the largest kite in the world, steering it in the sky above.

I was always annoyed by the sweat that would collect between my hand and my aunt's, as she held on to me tightly so that I wouldn't jump off like a grasshopper in front of her and get lost. The whole welfare thing didn't concern me, and I didn't even know what it meant until I asked my aunt about the significance of that office, and she replied: "This is Palestine." Or perhaps I'm making things up. My head was full of fantasies and I saw myself holding on to kites in all directions, and all the kites surrounded Palestine.

For a long time, I fantasized about Palestine and I would look forward to my aunt's arrival so that we could go and wander around the camp as usual, awaiting the opening of the welfare office. I was special in my aunt's eyes, since I was the one who struggled to utter a single syllable. I appeared unbalanced to her and didn't behave like the other children. In her opinion, I was too short and suffered from an unwillingness to progress beyond the age of six. In fact, I don't remember any of that. I only remember the arrival of the moment I had been waiting for, namely standing in a long line with my aunt to receive the welfare handout. At that moment, I understood that I was on the verge of entering a large amusement park called Palestine. I imagined cotton candy everywhere. I waited in silence for a long time with my aunt until it was our turn to enter. When we went in, I was overcome by dizziness and nausea.

I fell to the ground and everyone thought I had died. But I was at rest inside my head. The office was extremely ugly and the air was sparse in that room. Where was the colorful amusement park that I imagined? The images of rice, shortening, and egg cartons made me want to die more.

I was dead for a long time, two days. Everyone cried over me, including my aunt, who felt guilty for exhausting my body on that trip.

While I was dead, I roamed around Palestine. An old man with a white beard came along and picked me up and said: "Palestine has eyes of gold, but it doesn't like those who complain."

I rose up from the dead and went back to jumping around like a grasshopper, only to find myself daydreaming again.

All I ever wanted was to get a big balloon, tie it to the camp, and take it far away from here. The "here" is what suffocates me. Frankly, sometimes I can't tolerate the crush of so many people in one place. But I prefer not to express

my discomfort because it seems to me a total luxury to artic-
ulate an abhorrence for something that you have no ability to
change. My friend 'Ali tells me that power lies in expressing,
not changing. Of course, I disagree, and despite the fact that
he's a first-class hashish smoker and an expert when it comes
to women and politics, I can outdo him in my extraordinary
ability to puncture any seemingly well-reasoned idea and
turn it into a flight of fancy. In my humble opinion, complaining doesn't get you anywhere. There is no expressing
without changing, and no changing without expressing. It's
a knotty and sensitive issue.

Every day, I remind myself that I wasn't born to be
ordinary; I'm the camp's Superman. 'Ali explained to me at
length his own theory about me. In his opinion, my problem
was that I didn't have a title. Only men had titles. When
the news of this rule hit me, I became mute for a long time,
after which I asked for change without directly articulating
my demands. I began to cut my hair like men, dress like
them, and refer to myself and my actions using the masculine gender.

Everyone tried to accommodate me, since I had a
very delicate health condition and they didn't want me to
die. As I was the only child in the household of Abu 'Adil
al-Sidawi, I was specially cared for. Abu 'Imad found a neutral name for me, which wasn't affiliated with Hamas or
Fateh or the Popular Front for the Liberation of Palestine.
I was named "'Abdul Jalil." For 'Ali, the change that I
effected as an individual within the community was nothing short of a revolution, and he considers me distinctive in
my commitment to having freedom as a woman in a very
masculine world.

But I don't believe a word of it. I think that he over-does the analysis in proportion to the amount of hashish that he smokes. It's simpler than that—I just wanted a leg-endary title, like Superman, whom I consider more of a ref-ugee than myself. I wanted the title and I imagined myself walking alongside Superman. I imagined us smiling to each other. It was a magical thing for me to become a hero. I don't understand why it's necessary for everyone to be either a man or a woman. Why not simply be a hero.

'Ali says that I lost my femininity and that he alone is capable of retrieving it. I don't understand why he contin-ually needs to breathe close to my lips and, frankly, I don't like the smell of his breath much. I feel like I'm suffocating every time he reaches his hands toward my breast and turns to face me. Each time, my mother comes to my rescue. As for me, I'm incapacitated and powerless. I find myself stand-ing, waiting for something to happen. I don't object to 'Ali moving before me like a snake; I do nothing about it. As for my mother, she screams, cries, and rains down curses and obscenities at 'Ali and at the camp, and even at my father for good measure.

Then she holds my hand and shouts at me to make me understand that this is shameful. I really don't know what shame is. I don't want to know. I shut my ears and try to fan-tasize again. I'm not too inclined to stay close to my mother, since she never ceases to criticize me, even as she loses her fingers in the cushions while stuffing them with pieces of colored cloth. According to her, I'm going to bring shame on her because I hang out with the men in the square, and no one will marry me because they will see me as one of those who've been preyed upon. Quite simply, my mother is not entertaining. She isn't inspired like me by the world of ants and she's indifferent to my musings on space, which disappears between the wires that extend from house to house and behind the new floors that keep trying to reach higher, as though they don't want to stay on this earth.

I cried a lot when my father died. For the first time, I felt as though there was a woman stirring inside of me who felt the loss. I placed my hands on my breasts, I felt the curve of the pomegranate, and I entered my room as a man only to emerge again as a noisy woman.

No one understood the bout of craziness that struck me, but I realized that death itself had made me feel the necessity of changing again. I had many dreams in which I saw my father telling me that I was his daughter who resembled the moon. He didn't specifically say the word "moon," but I felt from the way he looked at me that I was his little beauty.

Time in that restricted space didn't pass easily. My mother stopped talking. She just prayed repeatedly everywhere, even in the bathroom, where she would call on God in her nakedness to rescue her from something I didn't understand. Maybe from her feelings of loss, fear, and loneliness, or maybe because she apprehended my yearning to leave.

I had started to grow up, and the city of devils, as my mother called it, began to twinkle in my eye. The old woman agreed to me leaving the camp to complete my university studies in Beirut on one condition: that I accompany her, every day for a whole month, on a journey by foot from the camp to the Uza'i shore, south of Beirut. I quickly agreed and we made a secret pact. Every day we would walk through the alleys of the camp in silence, passing all the faces that recognized us, emerging from one maze into another. My eyes would record each scene before me like a camera. Sometimes I felt as though I would cry again, but then I would remember that I abhor crying and wailing, along with all types of endless drama.

This camp is one of those worlds that seem to inhabit the clouds. No one sees it and it sometimes doesn't see itself. I ask questions and my questions slam pointlessly into the walls of each alleyway and bounce back to me. Mother, who put us in the clouds? I try to glean a single answer from her. The woman never responds. She's also been transformed, as I was. She's an absent presence and has no need to linger long, nor to leave.

We arrive at the Uza'i shore by foot. I don't feel tired; I feel nothing. The old woman throws herself down on the ground, as though she wants to return to it. My mother would like to inhabit the ground. All of her resentment and loathing for poverty has already been expressed, and she no longer has the ability to blame anyone. Her husband has died, and now I'm on the verge of abandoning her. She knows that God is her only solution, so she talks to him about everything, and when she grows tired she sleeps without stirring.

At the seashore, as the stench of the sewers infiltrates my nose, the old woman goes back to being a child. She plays with her little feet and sings softly to the sea: "Oh sea, take me back to my folks, swallow me and carry me. Oh sea, bring back my missing people, so that I can sleep in their laps, and forget all my cares."

We spend two hours in that place, then return to the camp. We look like two lost women. I don't resemble her, but I've begun to see her more clearly as I grow older. As we chase our shadows while we walk, I imagine how this old woman will die. Will the family grave be big enough for her too? I'm overcome by the shivers again and I remember: I don't want to be buried here. I want to die in Acre.

The camp was drowning in silence. The war that had occurred in the camp of Nahr al-Barid seemed to be lying in wait for us. All the faces were grimacing in anticipation of something happening. Many of the people from Nahr al-Barid had fled to Burj. One morning Umm Tawfiq told us the whole story of what happened there. Everyone gathered around to listen to her tale. She said: "All the camps will be finished off soon, everyone is conspiring against us, and we need to go . . ." "Where should we go?" my mother asked. "We should go back to our country. We should walk there the same way we came. Nahr al-Barid is gone and all the other camps will follow, there's no hope. They said they wanted to set us straight. We should just walk back." She explained how a Lebanese army officer had refused to let her take her own couch: "I shouted at him and said, this is my couch, what's wrong with you? It seems you don't know what Palestinian women are like." She took a knife, cut open the couch, and drew out some money that she had hidden inside. Then she looked at the officer and said: "This is my money." When Umm Tawfiq speaks, her stories get lost in constant digressions. She said she remembered the entire Nakba, even though she was very little when she left Palestine with her father.

In Nahr al-Barid, she saw people fleeing and screaming: "They even forgot their shoes." When they reached the camp, they sat on the sidewalk in the main street and saw the shells coming down on their houses. "Everything seemed clear to us. We were the ones being bombarded, not the houses." Umm Tawfiq's husband died in the war. When she speaks about it, disjointed laughs escape from her mouth: "I don't know, they say that my husband is a martyr. All I know is that he died and left me wandering from camp to camp like a cat." She describes how her husband, Abu Tawfiq, stood in front of a Lebanese tank, shouting: "You'll have to enter over my dead body." He didn't complete the sentence but fell to the ground like a hero. I ask myself: Why do these stories get replayed for us Palestinians? Why are we always supposed to die like that? We're either standing in a temporary land or hiding in an occupied land. Abu Tawfiq's body was abandoned in the heat of the sun for around half an hour. The world seemed to be drowning in the shock of that event.

The people of al-Burj camp tried to swallow the crisis of Nahr al-Barid camp, as they had tried to swallow the Nakba. As I walked around the camp, the weight of the stories would block my path from one alley to another. I tried to persuade myself that our country was not growing more distant, since I was the country; each one of us was a mobile country. But I couldn't remain silent. I walked to the cemetery at night and when I got there I couldn't stop screaming.

I felt as though I was completely absent, as in death, before I woke up to the sight of faces I knew. People's hands were warm and the cold water that they scattered on my face made me feel as though I needed to get up again. I was carried to Haifa Hospital and everyone stood around with my mother.

"It's just a nervous breakdown due to what's happening in Nahr al-Barid and the shitty situation we're in," was Dr. Fahmi's diagnosis. I would have liked to disappear. I just wanted to quench the fires lodged in my throat and imagination. I wanted to walk far from the camp. Maybe I was afraid that it too would disappear.

I pack my bags at dawn. I open my mother's room and notice that nothing has changed. Her prayer rug is folded on the chair, her bed is warm as usual, the smell of the room is as ancient as she is. I close the door and listen to her performing her ablutions before prayer. I sense a pain in my heart. I imagine a white shuttle on a loom entwining my body and carrying me away from all my doubts. I listen to her repeated invocations, then shut my ears. "God is great," she says; "God is great," I say. I yawn. I remember being with my aunt when I was little. She draws me close to her, runs her hand through my short hair, and reads the Qur'an. She says to me: "There's an evil eye on you." I yawn as a flood of tears flows out of her eyes. I think of my aunt as my fingers count the books that I will carry to my small apartment in Beirut. The apartment resembles a can of sardines. A sardine can in the city. I'm going to put the whole city in a sardine can, since I don't like cities. I'm going to search in the city for a road that would take me back to the beginning of the story, to Palestine. I may hide the camp in my hand. I laugh and my mother continues her prayers. I think of my aunt's face again. I recall how before her death she put her head on my knee and said: "I swear I'm confused, my little one. Are you a boy or a girl? When are you going to become a girl?" I remained silent and opted to imagine her floating in the sky above the camp, as though she were going to perform a pilgrimage in space.

My aunt died, just as many others in the camp had died before her. Few of the faces I know remain. My mother says:

"Time is like the blink of an eye. It cheats you and passes by quickly."

I pack my bags, arranging the books that I love: Kundera, Márquez, Ghassan Kanafani, Mahmud Darwish, Kafka, Lorca, and the Bible and Qur'an. There is a picture of Abu Jihad and another of Marlon Brando. I wear my translucent blue shirt and wait until the camp bustles with activity.

I go over to my mother, still sitting on her prayer rug. I gaze at her and she gazes at me, then I walk calmly to the door.

It's been some time since the old woman and I stopped conversing. That has relieved me. I won't go back, I say to myself. When I pass the torn posters on the walls of the camp, the martyrs seem to say goodbye to me, and the words of Abu 'Ammar appear before my eyes and remind me of my father. I look up at the electricity wires that I always dreamt about, jumping from one wire to another like Tarzan. Here is Ahmad's house, who died a couple of days ago in an electrical accident. At the door of the mosque, Abu Zuhdi stands pointing his rifle at Ihab the drug dealer, issuing threats against all those who traffic pills inside the camp. Close to the shop of Abu Tammam, who sells nuts, there has been an incident between young men belonging to Hamas and Fateh. The two factions have been fighting over the issue of posters and how to divide up the wall space fairly among them.

Everything here makes me laugh. It looks nothing like the homeland. But it tastes sweet and has a strange flavor, sometimes sharp. It's all normal, everything is normal. There's nothing wrong with living outside of time for a while. As my father used to say, "Everything outside Palestine is outside of time. There is no time outside Palestine." Never mind. I carry on, preventing myself from crying. I hate the wailing and the drama, and all manner of complaining. Not to worry, I observe space, which is covered by wires that appear to me like entrails, or rather like an assortment of veins. Who hung our veins here? The maze gives me a headache and makes me dizzy, and nausea strikes again.

I climb into the taxi. "Where to?" asks the driver. "To Palestine, I want to breathe." The taxi driver laughs and says: "Climb in, sister, you seem bored like me."

The Babbling of a Refugee

(b. Beirut, 1991)

What brought you here?

The heart led me somewhere I know not.

And how did you cross the border?

I don't remember crossing any border, I was just asleep.

And what did you dream about?

I dreamt that I returned to our house.

And where is your house?

In northern Palestine, east of the Mediterranean, I follow the waves to the old city of Acre.

Suddenly the conversation stops and a kick transports me into another world. At first, I thought it was delivered by the foot of the interrogator, but it was followed by a clear pronouncement: "Get up and go to school, you brute." There was no doubt about it—it was my father, and it was time for my daily journey of hardship to begin.

As was her usual habit, my mother had crumbled some *ka'k* for me in a bowl, poured milk over it, and sprinkled some sugar on top. She hid it deftly from my father, who always admonished her for adding sugar to my food.

My usual daily routine was to enter the hallway and wait until I heard the sound of our rickety metal door slamming shut, which would tell me that my father had left for work. Then I would take my turn in the bathroom, singing to myself while drumming along on the water jug. My mother would hurry me along, to make way for the convoy of my four siblings who were waiting in line. At last, I would emerge and devour the bowl of ka'k. Then the voices of the neighborhood kids outside would begin to beckon me to go to school with them, which was a two-kilometer walk from the camp.

Only Saturday was different because it was my father's day off. That day, there would be no singing in the bathroom, no sugar on the food, and no voices calling my name. To try to avoid detection by my father, my friend Ahmad and I would agree on a password for him to use instead of my name when he reached our neighborhood. He might call out, "Beeeep Beeeeeep," and I would know that he was waiting in the alleyway outside our house. I'd scramble out quickly before my father could discover he was there and holler out curses and damnation upon him. But the password could only be used twice, at most, before my father would figure it out. As soon as little Ahmad caught sight of big Ahmad's face, he would flee from the neighborhood, and my father would turn to me and utter his notorious sentence: "Damn the hour that I first saw you."

Of course, when I was born here in Burj al-Barajneh refugee camp, it wasn't my choice. I never invited my father to the second floor of Haifa Hospital. I wasn't yet able to move my finger to point to him and choose him as my father. It was my grandfather who whispered the call to prayer into my ear. I don't know if my father was even there.

While I tossed and turned in my mother's womb, no one consulted me to find out which country I wanted to belong to; I didn't have an identity card. Even the seed's entry into my mother's womb was coincidental. It was just an accident. My mother says that she was taken by surprise by her third pregnancy and that she didn't want it. My father had just been released from prison with a spent body and a new and difficult temperament. She was working, while he was recovering from the blows of his jailers. Why was this child being born at a time like this?

The Jinn

In the evenings, a garbage bag awaited me in front of the door to our house. My father refused to dispose of it in the neighborhood like our neighbors did, so I was supposed to carry the bag to the "dump," which surrounded the camp at all entrances. In the beginning, I would leave the house and turn right, heading in the opposite direction from the dump, and would toss the bag into the first deserted alleyway I found. But my father, with his uncanny intuition, soon found out about that, and disaster struck. My day turned into hell and ended with my skin turning shades of red and green from the lashes of his belt and cane against it.

I soon found another solution: our house looked out onto an abandoned house and, the distance between houses in our neighborhood being about an arm-and-a-half's length, I started throwing the bags into one of its open windows. Then I would occupy myself outside for a short while, corresponding to the time it would take to walk to the garbage dump.

Our neighbor Su'ad, who lived on the other side of the abandoned house, scolded me numerous times, but I ignored her as long as she didn't threaten to tell my father. But Su'ad, a woman in her forties living with her husband and four children, was smarter than I was, and she once invited me into her home and told me a story about the house next door. She told me that a tribe of jinn lived there.

I was unimpressed by Su'ad's story at first. But as evening fell and the camp went dark, due to the usual power cuts, Su'ad's words came back to me. I was suddenly seized by fear. The room that my siblings and I slept in, alternating head to toe so that we would fit, looked directly out over the abandoned house. I tossed and turned in my bed and couldn't get to sleep. I went over and glanced out of the window and saw shadows moving inside the abandoned house. I could hear gasping voices coming from the darkened rooms. I thought they sounded like the voices of people being tortured.

I called over my brother, 'Ali, who verified what I saw, and we both couldn't sleep that night. We spent all night observing the shadows crisscrossing the walls, trembling with fear. All this was happening in a house that nobody lived in, nobody slept in, and nobody even dared enter. At least, that's what my mother said the next morning when we explained what we'd seen. She dismissed everything we told her.

The next day, we gathered the neighborhood kids. We told them the story of the haunted house and what 'Ali and I had witnessed during the night. I embellished it by saying that the jinn had threatened to kidnap all the children in the camp, and 'Ali swore that I was telling the truth. No one called us out—Mustafa even said that he, too, had seen the jinn many times and Jamal confirmed this. We all determined not to go near the abandoned house and my friends pleaded with me not to throw any more garbage bags into it.

The garbage didn't pose a problem for long. I soon started throwing it onto the roof of Su'ad's house. To me, it seemed like a logical and conclusive solution. The roof was high and the stairs leading up to it had been largely destroyed by ancient mortar shells that had fallen upon it. Su'ad was fearful of trying to climb those stairs and I had no fear of her children, should they have discovered the garbage, since my brother 'Ali was the strongest kid in the neighborhood.

After the meeting in which we discussed the jinn, I went to my friend Wasim, who was ten years older than me. I used to call him "dimwit," since he had never gone to school. He was twice my height but was not ashamed to hang out with me, and he would do whatever I wanted.

Our friendship had begun with a fight. He had slapped me on the back of the neck when I passed in front of his house, and I responded by preparing an ambush for him at the intersection leading to our house. I settled the score with an empty soda bottle to his head, which resulted in six stiches that are still visible on his scalp this very day. After that incident, I could use Wasim to defend me. He was the tallest boy in the neighborhood, and 'Ali was the strongest.

Anyway, I told Wasim that I had lost a one-thousand-lira bill in the abandoned house and I asked him to go and look for it, promising to split it with him if he found it. The offer was too tempting for him to decline, so he waited until nightfall to enter the house without being seen.

After it got dark, I watched him climb the stairs leading to the abandoned house. He showed no hesitation. But only a minute later, he ran back panting. His heart was beating fast and he made hurried circular motions with his arms to indicate that he wanted me to follow him. I wasn't prepared to do that, until he managed to splutter some choppy sentences conveying to me what he'd seen. I led the way there at once, having completely forgotten the whole issue of the jinn, just as Wasim had forgotten the one-thousand-lira note.

The door to the abandoned house was partly smashed and we poked our heads in through the corner of the frame to take a look. Inside was a large man with his back to the door, on top of a woman's body. He was naked from the waist up and we could see his bent spine and his head of thinning hair, moving rhythmically back and forth. I heard the very same gasping noises that I had heard the night before. Wasim's legs had given in and he was now kneeling in front of the door. I found a rock nearby and aimed it at a lantern inside that was casting a faint light on the scene. Darkness descended everywhere. I started running without knowing why I had done it, Wasim running behind me. I arrived at my house somehow and threw myself into bed.

I was perplexed and terrified by what I had seen. I thought it was the jinn that our neighbor had warned me about—a wicked jinn who brought women into his house and had sex with them.

Rations

When I was little, I used to hate being hungry. I would eat at short intervals so that I would never experience the feeling of hunger. When I couldn't get food, I would chew my lower lip until it got inflamed and infected. My mother said that I once caught a stomach bug that made me feel hungry all the time and drove me to eat a lot.

My father was an UNRWA employee; in fact, he still works as a security guard at their main offices. As a result, ours was the only house that didn't receive the UNRWA food rations that were distributed to all camp residents—even though we were the only ones who paid rent, while all the other families owned their homes. This latter wasn't any concern of mine; what did interest me were the tightly sealed food rations. I would go to Wazzan Square, where the rations were distributed, to see the great throng of people that formed there once a month. Some friends and I once climbed an electricity pole to get a glimpse of the action from above. We climbed right to the top and, as they began to count out the rations down below, I looked into the window of Abu Sa'id's house.

Inside was the most beautiful young woman in the camp. She was nearly twenty years old and I was just ten, though I always said ten and a half anyone asked. But for some reason I didn't think that age was a problem at all. I would close my eyes and find her beside me. I would take a strand of her long black hair, which spilled down her back, in my hand. Her shoulder was too far for me to reach, because of the difference in our heights. We would walk together along the road to the airport, which ran alongside the camp. A shout from below snapped me out of my dream: "Come down, you two, you're going to fall and break your necks!"

I looked down and saw Hajjeh A'isha underneath us brandishing a kitchen knife, waving it to warn us of the dangers of falling. The shadow she cast behind her covered the whole alleyway. Hajjeh A'isha was sturdily built and so fat that we would make fun of her as kids. I had two options: either come down and face Hajjeh A'isha's sharp knife, or stay up high and ogle the one I secretly named Sarah. Of course, I decided to ignore A'isha's shouts and continue to feast my eyes. But Sarah soon noticed me and shut her window snappishly, calling out: "I'm going to tell your parents!" One of my friends jumped down the pole in fear, only to be pursued by A'isha waiting below. I waited for the coast to be clear and ran away without being followed.

That day, I was afraid to go back home and dawdled for a long time between the al-Khazzan quarter, Sal'us quarter, and Dar Wardeh until nightfall. The rule was that I couldn't stay out after Hajj Safadi began the call to prayer at sunset. I had been suppressing my urge to pee all day. I had stopped myself from going in the road since I now considered myself a man who knew love, and a real man would never urinate in the road. As soon as I opened the door to our house, I was met with my father's voice: "Come here." I was confident that I'd done nothing wrong that day. I didn't get into a fight with anyone, I hadn't hit a single cat in sight of one of the neighborhood women, and I hadn't even thrown out the garbage bag, since it was a Saturday and the garbage didn't go out until Sunday evening. My only worry was that someone had told him about me spying on Sarah.

He asked me to bring him the hose that was used to connect the propane tank. It was a thick and sturdy blue hose, but it was flexible when wielded by my father against my back. In his hands, it became malleable, softened by warmth and perspiration. It even spoke the language that my father reserved exclusively for his three male offspring. I said: "Baba, what did I do?" And he replied: "Will you bring the hose, or shall I?" Since I had some experience with that request, I chose to bring him the hose myself, and as soon as he received it, he asked me to turn around.

At that instant, I was overcome by the urge to pee and I begged him to let me go to the bathroom, but he had already started whipping. I cried out, but he just kept striking me without me knowing why, until I wetted myself. At that instant, the earth stopped turning for a few moments. His hand came to rest, more out of disgust at the stench of my urine than out of mercy.

Some women from the neighborhood were visiting that night and they witnessed the whole thing. I had to remove my pants and underwear, covered in urine, in front of them.

I rushed into the bathroom, sat down on the tiles, and recalled Sarah's round face, but this time it looked repulsive, because she was the reason for all this.

After a few minutes, I tried to open the bathroom door but was surprised to find it locked from the outside. When I banged forcefully on the door, my father got annoyed and turned the electricity off in the house. He knew very well that I was afraid of the dark, especially when I was in the bathroom. I begged him to open the door and was told firmly: "Count to a hundred."

But I'd always hated math and I could only count up to twenty in one go. I started counting. For me, thirty was close to twenty, it was practically its next-door neighbor. But for my father, it lived nine doors away.

That incident caused me to dislike numbers even more, as they led me to conjure all the jinn of the earth and do battle with them in the bathroom.

That night, I fell asleep and woke up lying next to my brother on a plastic sheet that my mother had laid down for me. She had poured water on me and washed me without me even feeling it. It was as though she was washing a corpse. Strangely enough, when I woke up, I slipped out of the house early and made my way back to Wazzan Square. I climbed the electricity pole and cast a glance toward the window of the Sa'id house, but it was closed this time and I never saw Sarah again.

Nation

Names are not arbitrary; they can't be. They always go to the heart of the matter. Often, they tell us things about people before we meet them. When you go to meet someone named "Abdullah," for example, you don't take a bottle of wine, whereas you might take one when you go to meet someone called "Joe." Some names are so rare that you need a red kufiyah to gain their intimacy.

A red kufiyah, steeped in blood from the first March of Return, a witness to the first stone to cross the border, and a companion to my first sight of the homeland. It was a kufiyah that expressed everything I wanted to say, so I carried it to her, and it conveyed my love. It was completely planned—it wasn't a coincidence that this young woman of Palestine should fall in love with me above all others. For her name was heavy and couldn't be shortened, and it was a name borne by no one else on this earth.

Before her, I was a contrary child who defied relatives, neighbors, and teachers. I knew nothing of love but the fake letters that I would write for my friends in return for money.

They admired my words about their girlfriends, words that meant nothing to me, nothing but the one thousand liras that I would get for each letter.

In high school, everything changed: something in my chest began to beat strongly. Her hair was reddish, her face was formed of the earth of the nation, her presence had a special luster. We were joined together in many patriotic activities; in the poetry and theatre through which she would call out to the homeland.

She gave me a Palestine chain, and I gave her a Hanzala keepsake, and everything that passed between us was sacred like the nation. She is far away now, since the fates drove me to seek my fortune in exile and brought me back again. They have not conspired to lead me back to her yet, but I have faith, just as the Sufi has faith in his master. I love her as I love the country that she was named after. But what have I done now? I've confessed everything but her name. Her name was "Watan" (Nation)!

Istanbul

The distance between the house and the train station was about half an hour's walk in the storm. We climbed a road leading uphill. The snow covered our feet and weighed down our legs as we raised and lowered them. Despite the icy roads, life around us had not calmed down and we were surrounded by a cacophony of sound. Children were sliding down the hills on kitchen trays. A young woman, inebriated by the storm, was frantically clinging to her boyfriend. An elderly man was entertaining his family with snowballs.

We took the train to the airport, where a strange scene was unfolding. Crowds of people had congregated, awaiting flights that had been delayed by hours. A blonde-haired woman had fallen asleep on a bench, her toes virtually touching the mouth of the man who accompanied her, without so much as disturbing his sleep.

Everyone was overcome with boredom. The airlines were distributing food to travelers, who stood in long rows in front of the display panels announcing the departures and arrivals. Suddenly, the agent distributing the food raised his voice and we gathered around to hear what he was saying. One of the passengers had touched him from behind, perhaps unintentionally, but the agent interpreted this as an assault, and tapped angrily on the passenger's back, yelling loudly in English: "You want this?!"

My brother and I laughed at the commotion. Soon after, we heard someone else shouting on the upper level. This time, it was some passengers demanding hotel rooms for the night since their flight had been delayed by over twelve hours. They yelled at the airline employees but privately they weren't annoyed; they were laughing among themselves.

* * *

After some hours of waiting, I was directed into the security screening room because I was carrying a travel document that the official was unable to decipher. He asked me: "Where are you from?" I replied, as I always did: "From Palestine." He glanced at my papers and then he looked back at me and said: "You're from Lebanon." I said: "I'm a refugee from Palestine to Lebanon." That was too difficult for him to grasp, so he turned me over to another security official, who said: "Where are you from." I replied: "From Palestine."

He held a magnifying glass up to his left eye, examined my document closely, then looked at me and asked: "Are you going to Lebanon?" I said, "Yes." He said: "So you're from Lebanon." I replied: "No, I'm from Palestine; I'll live in Lebanon until such time as I return to my land." I don't think he understood, and I couldn't explain the whole question of Palestine in a matter of minutes, from the Balfour Declaration to the displacement that led to my exile. But he accepted my documents and ushered me on my way.

The gate leading to Palestine was numbered 220. Every time I entered a foreign airport I made sure to search for the planes flying to my home country, and this time there was one just a few steps away from my own gate. The sign said "Tel Aviv," so my feet carried me to that gate, where dozens of passengers stood glued to the glass windows, watching the heavily falling snow, and cursing their bad luck. Everyone was waiting, but waiting had a different meaning at the gate leading to Palestine.

When I arrived at 220, the employee blocked my path: "Where are you from?" "From Palestine." He saw the Palestine chain that I always wore around my neck and asked for my papers, then he directed me to go to gate 227.

When we boarded the plane, I met a woman in her sixties who asked me if she could have my window seat, so I gave it to her. She said: "Where are you from?" I said: "From Palestine." She smiled, replying: "Where in Palestine, my dear?" I said: "From Acre, *hajjeh*." So she said: "Blood is thicker than water, my son, I'm from Jaffa." We had a long conversation during which I learned that she had Lebanese citizenship, though if you asked her where she was from, she would immediately reply: "I'm from Jaffa, bride of Palestine."

The plane engine was loud and the woman from Jaffa was playing a game on her tablet. From time to time, she would ask me to help her, and I would decline, since I don't play games at all, and she would just smile at me. The plane took off and the lady let out a frightened cry because of the heavy turbulence. Once the plane was flying above the clouds, the woman smiled at me again, patted me on the shoulder, and said: "I swear by this sun," pointing out the window, "which I haven't seen for five days, that when you get married, I'm going to buy your wife her wedding dress."

Openness

Things are no longer what they used to be. I walk along the seashore in Beirut and look inward. If you conversed with me a little, you might think that I'm not the child who once wandered night and day through the camp. But if you really befriended me, you'd soon discover that I'm one and the same, and you'd recognize some of the scars and bruises that my body retains to this day, or some of the blemishes left upon my soul.

I'll tell you a secret: I still chase my shadow at noon, as I did when I was a kid. Every night, I pick out the ten most beautiful stars in the sky, and I bite on my lower lip when I'm hungry. I still visit the sea as often as I can, and I'm still thrilled by the reddening of the sun at sunset. This is all the same and my country is still the same: truthful and false, near and far, beautiful and ugly, loyal and treacherous, strong and weak.

But everything else has changed. I'm no longer frightened by the jinn, having made his acquaintance, and the garbage is no longer my daily priority. Even the interrogator has softened his tone with me—my answers and my features are familiar to him now.

I walk along the seashore at twilight with my eyes on the horizon, with my hands behind my back and my tongue hidden inside my mouth. Her voice comes to me suddenly. "A great joy awaits you, which shines through your sad eyes," she said, as she surreptitiously tried to read my palm. "Your luck is controlled by a star in the sky," she added, trying to entangle me in her plot. I remained silent, but spread out my hand in surrender. She froze, then took a gulp of air, and recovered her ability to speak after a moment of silence. "There's a difficult girl in your life. The bridges between you are broken. Things will improve, but time moves like the hands of a clock, and everyone will have their day. The path in front of you begins in fire and ends in roses." I smiled, and she continued: "Don't harbor any fear of her in your heart, for she loves you like no one else does!" I smiled more broadly and drew her fee from my pocket. She said: "Give her my regards." I said: "Who?" She replied: "Your homeland!"

Ever since I Became a Mother, I've Hated Winter

NADIA FAHED

(b. Sharjah, 1987)

Despite my avid love of swimming in the sea in summertime, I prefer—or, rather, I used to prefer—winter. Not for its romantic ambience, its intimacy, or its poetic qualities, and not because I enjoy walking in the rain, but for the sole reason that in winter, insects would disappear from the camp!

But ever since I became a mother, I've hated winter. I hate it because it's turned into a curse, a bother, and a burden. It's become a routine source of worry and disquiet for me. With every rainy morning, I must go through the process of selecting the most appropriate plan to exit the house and make my way to my parents' place, or my in-laws', to drop off my nursing daughter, Qamar, before heading to work. Even though our houses are only separated by a six- or seven-minute walk, in winter the trip takes an eon.

I carry her, all bundled up in layers to protect her from the rain, in one hand, while carrying the umbrella in the other. As we like to say, *Kull ishi tamam*, "It's all good."

I head toward the main road, traversing the alleyways, my footsteps quickening until I'm nearly jogging. The road is where the problem lies. Motor scooters speed like lightning bolts in all directions, carrying women, children, and men. They flow steadily forward, while me, my daughter, and the umbrella are just another barrier in the way of their deluge.

I'm forced to take a step back to let someone pass from one alley to the next, or I find myself having to close the umbrella halfway with one hand to let someone else have right of way. I feel embarrassed when someone is kind enough to let me pass, and I forge ahead, taking with me an assortment of things that stick to the umbrella, including hair, clothes, and limbs.

I was soon compelled to buy a special backpack carrier for small infants—what's sometimes known as a "kangaroo bag," a truly ingenious invention for any mother or father. Once one of my hands had been liberated, at least part of my problem was solved—or so I thought. The alleyways had a different idea.

Picture this: Qamar is in the "kangaroo bag" and I'm carrying the umbrella, charging confidently against the wind. I'm suddenly pulled back by a violent force. The umbrella is yanked from my hand. I look back and find that it's hooked on the low-lying electricity wires and water pipes. So I go back to extract it carefully, bracing myself for an electric shock.

I'm seized by phobias and recall all the cases of death by electric shock that have occurred in the camp, due to the chaotic intermingling networks of electrical wires and water pipes. What if I get zapped by the electrical current? Would it reach the body of my daughter underneath her layers of blankets, God forbid? How would I react and what would I do? I banish all these thoughts and surrender to the fates.

You might be wondering: why am I going to all this trouble? Why not just use a stroller? I've already tried that. The roads in the camp are shot to pieces, unfit for human transport, especially during the rainy season. The routes to my parents' and my in-laws' houses are relatively long, and are full of bizarre geological formations, mounds, slides, hills, cliffs, inclines, and precipices. But the larger issue is how to carry the stroller up the three flights of stairs to my apartment. There's no elevator in my building and not enough space or security to leave the stroller on the ground floor.

It would seem that the only way out for me and Qamar is for my husband to get a motor scooter. But since my husband and I are creatures of "etiquette," as some like to describe us, we refuse to transport her by scooter when she is just a nursing infant. We insist on carrying her through the bug-infested alleyways in summertime to avoid putting her on a motorbike. You can only imagine my husband's mortification, and my own, when I scream and hop around like a crazy person whenever I suddenly encounter a cockroach in my path. This happens especially in the evenings, when the cockroaches take over in all their glory. I hate bugs and I hate that I hate them!

My late grandmother, may she rest in peace, always relied on me to help her bathe, to her utter misfortune and mine. Before bath time, I would always send my mother on a reconnaissance mission to check the bathroom for cockroaches or other insects. The crawlspace in my grandmother's bathroom was somehow connected to the neighbors' roof. Don't ask me how—the architecture of houses in the camp is a real wonder. But that meant that it was a gateway for those repulsive insects.

After ascertaining that the coast was clear, it was my turn to carry out maneuvers. I would grasp the end of the mop and position myself as far away as possible from the door to the bathroom, standing on tiptoe. There I would shake and rattle the mop repeatedly, creating as much of a din as possible, giving my enemy a chance to exit the battlefield. At that point, I would draw closer to the bathroom, repeating my maneuver again, and then, and only then, would I give my grandmother the green light to approach. The bathing would begin as usual, and it would soon produce in us the familiar sensations of asphyxiation and claustrophobia. The space was scarcely large enough for both of us, and with the door closed I felt captive, without an escape route if a cockroach appeared from nowhere. It was a real source of horror for me, and my poor grandmother could feel my anxiety and sense of urgency. But she never realized that what lay behind it was my fear of bugs, not my lack of interest in helping her bathe or my distaste for it. I never dared tell her the truth. I would have felt extremely silly saying, "I'm afraid that the cockroaches will come, *sitti*." She was the type simply to swipe them aside with her hand. Just like that, as though they were flies.

To make things worse, my grandmother was a loyal enthusiast of locally made soap, especially the kind made of olive oil, and she resolutely shunned the use of any other product on her hair. Washing her hair with a bar of soap took a long time, adding to my suffering and multiplying my anxiety. But my efforts to cajole her to use shampoo were all in vain.

As the water quality in the camp deteriorated and turned saltier, my grandmother began to tire of the endless effort to scrub her hair with soap without working up a lather. She finally surrendered to the shampoo option. I had been waiting for that moment for an eternity. But she soon reversed her decision when her skin had an allergic reaction to, as she put it, "that filthy shampoo that you all use."

Of course, that was only to be expected from a woman who had spent her whole life using natural soap, and who had even made her own soap when she was still in good health. I remember her preparing a batch of soap on the roof, in a large pot over a wood fire. She let it boil then poured it into a metal mold divided into smaller cubes, telling me and my siblings not to play in the vicinity. She had one eye on us and the other on her various potted plants distributed around the roof.

We could never understand why she went to all that trouble in the twentieth century, when soaps of all colors and varieties were at our fingertips. As children, we didn't appreciate how enlightened her behavior was, and how utterly wholesome and ecological. Medical research is constantly warning us nowadays about the dangers and hazards of soaps and shampoos that contain all kinds of chemical additives.

My grandmother was way ahead of us. All of her daily routines were friendly to the environment. She always sewed her own clothes and reused and recycled pieces of cloth. She hated using paper tissues and saved empty containers, glass jars, and plastic bags.

Her habits didn't come from a delusional impulse that afflicts the elderly, or a phobia about losing stuff, or an obsession with hoarding. It was an instinctive love for the land and the spirit of village and country life that lived in my grandmother, having been born and raised in the village of Shaykh Dawud in the District of Acre.

Even though my grandmother had taken us back to square one when it came to the bathing ritual, I was determined not to surrender. I began to put a small dollop of shampoo in her hair, without her noticing, before she scrubbed it with soap and combed it. As far as I was concerned, it was a compromise that assuaged me and left her satisfied.

I always worried about transmitting my fear of cockroaches to my daughter Qamar. So far, for reasons that I can't fathom, she has no trace of it. She's scarcely perturbed when she sees a cockroach passing by. Instead, she gets excited and races over to crush it with her foot, as a thin smile plays over my mouth. The smile is my attempt to hide my horror. The last thing I want is for my daughter to seize upon my weakness and use it to blackmail me or to get what she wants—a bar of chocolate, for example.

I've hated cockroaches ever since I was little and, because of that, would take pains to torture them. Whenever I'd see one flipped on its back in the hallway of our house or on the roof, I would light a candle and pour the molten wax, drop by drop, onto it, transforming it into a petrified wax statue.

I once came across the information that a cockroach is the only living being that would survive a nuclear bomb, and that it can live for ten days without a head. Yet more reasons to hate and dread that revolting creature.

I remember once engaging in a conversation about the supernatural and the fate of animals on the Day of Judgement, especially those that had been tortured by humans. A friend of mine claimed that animals would wreak their revenge on those who had harmed them, using the same means. That gave me a fright. Did it apply to insects too? What a disaster. Can you imagine a human-sized cockroach retaliating against you? Wouldn't that be pure hell?

By contrast with cockroaches, I've always had a fascination with ants. Whenever I found them on the roof or near various cracks in the house, I'd make sure to sprinkle some sugar for them. Sometimes I would observe them closely until I fell asleep, then wake up and find that they had accomplished their mission of retrieving all the sugar I'd left, grain by grain. I got very upset with my mother for asking my father to fill up all those cracks with caulk, so as to be rid of the ants and all the dirt they brought in from their ant kingdom. At the same time, I was confident that they'd always find a way to reopen the cracks or find new outlets. When I was especially bored, I might help them reopen the cracks.

Most of the houses in the camp were originally built on sandy soil. In the beginning, there were temporary tents, followed by small rooms built out of clay and straw, with tin roofs, and, finally, the architectural misfits of today. These were only constructed as a result of a long struggle to bring building materials into the camp.

My grandmother laid the first stone for our house, just as everyone else did in our neighborhood and other parts of the camp. They built their houses themselves, without any planning or engineering, or any help of any kind. They did so with their blind faith and whatever came to hand. My grandmother gathered discarded building materials from the camp's surroundings, or collected leftovers from construction sites farther afield. She'd come back from these forays with a variety of different tiles in all shapes and colors. The floors of our rooms were like mismatched mosaics. When we'd make fun of the variegated floors, she'd reply decisively, and with a measure of pride: "We were the first to tile our floors; other people used to pour concrete." We were often surprised to find tiles in the same style on the floor of a friend's or neighbor's house. We'd say: "*Sitti* just needed that one tile to complete the pattern in our house."

Above ants, my greatest passion is for cats. Not just any cats—the camp's cats. I prefer them to foreign cats, or as we like to say, "bourgeois cats." Our home was never cat-less. I raised them either inside the house or on the roof.

I've had many weird cats, but the weirdest of all brought me gifts and rewards, believe it or not. At least, that's what they must have seemed like from the cat's point of view.

His name was Mushu and he was insane. He'd move hysterically between the rooms, playing and amusing himself. He'd dart up to the roof like a rocket, disappearing for a short time, then race back down carrying some reward. One night, he set off as usual and came back with a dead bird. I think he was trying to impress me with his hunting skills, but it was clear that the bird was dead when he found it because it already looked desiccated. I ignored him, so he launched again like a rocket, returning with another bird. This time, I scolded him, and he laid down and curled himself up in a ball. Suddenly, he sprinted away again, coming back this time with a cockroach, which he spat out in front of me. How totally gross! Thankfully, the cockroach was in its death throes and scarcely moving, as I recall.

After a severe reprimand and a period of shunning from me, he dropped the habit. But then, several nights later, he startled me with a rabbit! I was fast asleep when I felt Mushu jump onto my bed carrying a creature in his mouth, which he proceeded to deposit right next to me. It felt heavy and my heart nearly stopped with fear that night. I only found out what it was when I sprang up to turn the light on and made out that it was a mature live rabbit, almost the size of Mushu himself. I was stunned, but I have to admit that I was also quite delighted. I hugged Mushu and kissed him: "Who's a pretty boy? What a lovely sight! Wherever did you get him from? How in the world were you able to carry him?" Later on, I learned that the rabbit belonged to our neighbor, but I never owned up, and I raised him as though he had always been mine.

Qamar is also enamored of cats. She loved to visit my grandmother's house, where a number of stray cats would always settle. It was calm and safe for them there. They became used to the place and to us visitors, never flinching or scampering off when they saw us. My grandmother always enjoyed our visits and was happy to see us; it was as though life had been restored to her. One time she surprised me when she was playing with Qamar and I heard her say: "Qamar, my little bunny, come get a coin."

What?! I was dumbfounded. I thought she only used that nickname with me. I was convinced it was exclusively reserved for me, my private name. It was always accompanied by a little jingle that she gently clapped along to: "I hope you never die, my dear, and don't lie in your grave in fear."

It distresses me now that Qamar won't remember my grandmother and has no special memories of their time together. But I know that I'll tell her so many stories and anecdotes about her. She was only a year and a half old when my grandmother passed away. I still find it hard to accept the reality of her death. I can't bring myself to visit her grave.

I hate the thought of her being there. It's not that I object to God's will and judgement, nor do I doubt that death is real, but it fills me with pain, anger, and sadness. How could she have died in exile, still dreaming of returning to her land until her last breath, only to be buried as a refugee in a strange land?

Even dead refugees should have the right to return to Palestine. My grandmother's body should return there, to her village. I doubt that this is a concern of our Palestinian leadership but, as a refugee, I declare that the return to Palestine is every refugee's right, dead or alive.

My grandmother was constantly preoccupied with staying in touch with her relatives in her village of Shaykh Dawud. When she was still alive, telecommunications weren't as advanced as they are now. The central telephone exchange was her only means of contacting and asking after them. I'd accompany her there whenever she asked me to. I don't know why she insisted on going very early, or why I would agree, especially since I would be the one who was put on the spot. I would have to knock on the door of the home of the telephone operator and wake him up. "My grandmother would like to speak to her family in Palestine; it's urgent, please." I think that if he hadn't been so taken aback by this request, he might have rebuked me for disturbing him so early in the morning.

Then I would go to the telephone exchange, which was just a few steps away from his house, where my grandmother was waiting.

"Isn't he there, *sitti*?"

"Yes, he is, but I told you he'd still be asleep, it's still early. He's just getting himself ready and will be here soon."

Then, he would show up: "Welcome, welcome, Umm Khayr, please come in, *hajjeh*."

"How are you, my dear? May God be pleased with you and ease your path. How are your mother and father, dear?"

Once inside, she'd hand me her telephone book, and I would search for the number of Abu Ibrahim, or anyone else with her family name, then I would pass it to the man to dial the number. That's how she would find out how they all were, who got married, who gave birth, and who died.

She spoke constantly about her life in Palestine. I often doubted some of the things she said, especially when it came to her family's ownership of land, the beauty of her house, the splendor of life there, and so on. I thought that it was the kind of exaggeration that comes with longing, yearning, and reminiscing.

But I later found out that everything she had said was an understatement. The details were all correct and accurate. It was actually more beautiful than her description and lovelier than my imagination.

I'm one of the fortunate few whom God graced with the chance to visit Palestine. Two of my friends and I decided that our "return" to Palestine would be lacking if we didn't "return" to the very same villages that our families had been displaced from. And that's what we did. Since we didn't have a permit from the occupation authorities to enter the territories occupied in 1948, we sought the help of a brave man from Jerusalem who smuggled Palestinian workers from the West Bank to the "inside." He knew the name of every village in Palestine by heart. As soon as I said I was from Shaykh Dawud, he recognized it and broke out into a smile, rattling off the names of several neighboring villages.

All we had to do was cross the "border" of the West Bank and pass through one of the Israeli checkpoints. The man from Jerusalem had a car with an Israeli license plate, which allowed him to enter and exit the West Bank. He told us to keep quiet, relax, and act natural, so as not to arouse any suspicions in case they stopped us at the checkpoint and asked for his car permit.

When we got to the first checkpoint, the soldiers asked him to step out of the car and bring the identity cards of everyone inside. "We're screwed!" we thought; this was supposed to be the easiest checkpoint. They started scrutinizing our documents. We tried to stay calm when we saw the man returning with one of the soldiers. The soldier handed back the papers, saying: "They can't go through, they need a permit."

He got back in the car. "They're not going to let us pass. Don't be upset, we'll go to another checkpoint and try." After many overt and covert prayers and incantations, the second checkpoint turned out to be less strict; the soldiers only asked for the car permit and waved us on. We finally managed to breathe a sigh of relief. We were on our way to fulfilling the dream of return!

We drove to Jaffa, then Acre. The names of the villages in the district of Acre began to appear. I could hardly contain myself when I saw the name of the village of Shaykh Danun, which neighbors and intertwines with the village of Shaykh Dawud. We didn't know what we were looking for—we only had the family name. When we arrived in Shaykh Danun, we asked the village butcher about the Fahed family. He motioned us to keep going uphill. All along the drive, I turned my head right and left to see if I could make out anything that resembled my grandmother's descriptions.

"Could this be it? No, that's not possible. Keep going a little farther." And a little later: "Wait, stop here. That must be them." I have no idea how I knew that that was the right spot. I just knew. It was as though I had known this house and its inhabitants for an eternity.

The car had stopped in front of a metal gate, behind which an elderly man and two women were sitting and sipping their afternoon coffee.

"Greetings, *hajj*. Is this the Fahed family house? We just want to make sure."

"Yes, my dear, welcome," was the surprised and apprehensive response from the elderly man. He looked at us as though we were a group of aliens who had just descended from a spaceship.

My God, I'm at my grandmother's house. I'm in my village. *I'm from here.* This is my house. This is where I'm meant to be. This is where I'm supposed to come every weekend and for my summer vacations. Why am I not here? Why am I over there, a refugee in a miserable camp in Lebanon?

I drew closer to them: "May God give you strength, I'm from Lebanon. I'm the daughter of Khayr Fahed. My grandmother is Umm Khayr Hussani." Her first name was Hussniyya, but Hussani was her nickname, after a type of bird with a sweet song, maybe because she had a beautiful voice and sang at weddings.

The old man breathed a long sigh and got up from his chair to hug me. "My dear, you carry the scent of the precious ones," he said, and we all started crying.

Dear Grandmother, life is tasteless in your absence. You left a large lump in my throat. It's a lump that hurts me and makes me choke. *Sitti*, I visited our village, Shaykh Dawud. I managed to slip past the occupiers. I met your relatives, my relatives. I told them about you, and they told me about you. And they related your common memories. I walked among our village's neighborhoods, I visited its shrine, and I read the opening prayer from the Qur'an for the soul of your martyred brother, Salih, about whom you told me many stories. I stood on the ruins of the house that you were born and grew up in. The setting was just as you described it, only lovelier.

The cruelty of fate is such that it denied you your simple wish to die in your own land. It terrifies me to think that I might die far away. Your grave should be there, not here, in forced exile in a refugee camp.

I promise you that one day, I'll sit beside your grave and read the opening prayer for your soul. But it'll be there, not here. There, where your favorite lemon tree still remembers you, misses you, and is waiting for you.

Da'uq: A Burial Plot, a Cemetery

(b. Beirut, 1957)

In the closet of my father, may he rest in peace, a tin bis-
cuit box and envelopes of various sizes were stored carefully. After the funeral proceedings and the condolences had
ended, I sat alone in front of his closet, the storehouse of
his secrets.

Here was the box where he had meticulously stashed
the family photographs. Some of these he had carried with
him from Palestine, while others had been taken in the
bloom of his youth. He was especially proud of the pictures
he had taken with Arab artists visiting Lebanon, where he
had migrated with his family. He had one with the Egyptian
comedian Hasan Fayiq and another with the actor Husayn
Sudqi. There were pictures of us as children on the occasion
of the outdoor festivals to celebrate 'Id. One photograph
showed a backdrop of the late Egyptian leader Jamal Abdul
Nasir with a hand outstretched to shake ours. These were
just some of the many pictures taken on various occasions.

The envelopes were scruffy like their contents: various
documents, birth certificates, and our report cards from elementary school. But the real treasure was an envelope that
had been carefully folded as though it contained a holy relic.
I opened it to find papers belonging to my grandfather, who
was an antique furniture merchant in Jaffa, including sales
invoices and rental contracts. It also held title deeds to my

great aunt's house and her Palestinian passport in its three languages, Arabic, English, and Hebrew.

My memory took me back to the story of my family's migration from Palestine, of their arrival in Beirut in a boat that was nearly destroyed before making it safely to shore. At first, they sought refuge with relatives of my grandmother, who was of Lebanese origin. They stayed with them for a short time and then moved on to various places, including a horse stable located between Jalloul and the Martyrs' Cemetery, before they settled at last in Da'uq, a burial plot in Beirut. The plot, no larger than thirty meters by forty, was donated by the Da'uq family to accommodate Palestinian refugees until they could return to their homes. It was bounded on the west side by Sabra Square and the Islamic Seniors' Home, and on the north side by Rawas Street.

Da'uq had a single main gate that opened onto the main street of Sabra. As residents tell it, before 1960 that gate was commanded and controlled by men from the Deuxième Bureau (of the Lebanese intelligence services). They would scrutinize all those who entered and left Da'uq, especially those traveling from faraway places, questioning them about their relationship with residents and the purpose of their visit, just to make things tougher for the people living there.

A row of shops served as a kind of wall for Da'uq. On one side of the main gate was Subhi al-Batal's shop, which sold candy and ice cream. He was my first customer—I made one lira from him for drawing the likeness of a boy with an ice-cream cone to hang on the side panel of his delivery bike. On the other side of the gate was Abu Muhammad al-Yassir's shop, where you could buy sandwiches of spleen, brains, and tongue, as well as alcoholic drinks. Abu Muhammad had his own special rituals. After preparing the varieties of meats, vegetables, and pickles, and lining them up methodically, he would pour himself a glass of arak and make his own special mezze, then he would light a cigarette and switch on the cassette player, blaring the voice of the "Eastern Star," Umm Kulthum. Only after sipping from his drink and preening himself would he begin to take his customers' orders. Next door to him was a shop selling ful, hummus, and fatteh, owned by Abu Mahmud, and nearby was an outfit that specialized in repairing and soldering shishas and kerosene heaters, owned by Abu Khalil al-Masalkhi. Next to them was a juice store belonging to a member of the Abu Husah family, then the Hammami supermarket and roastery, and two grocery stores, one owned by Abu Marwan and the other by Abu 'Adas. The latter had a window looking out onto our alleyway, from which he used to hand us our groceries. There was also a wholesale enterprise that sold grains and oils, which was the proud possession of Abu Taysir "al-Yazuri" (from the village of Yazur in Palestine). The al-Ittihad bookstore belonging to Yahya 'Ubayd was where we bought our stationery and greeting cards and also collected our mail. The best date sweets came from Abu 'Abd al-Ahwal, next door to the al-Salayhi Café where my grandfather and I shared our last cup of tea before his death. That day, it seemed as though he was taking a final tour of the neighborhood, visiting all the shopkeepers and his friends. We'd also bought some fine semolina, from which he would make 'asida sweets with his own hands. To the right was the al-'Ashi butcher shop and Fawzi 'Ubayd's radio and television repair shop.

There was another exit from Da'uq, which opened onto the "Aviation" area, so named because it was the site of the first airport established in Beirut, near the current Cité Sportive stadium. But entry and exit to Da'uq was largely through the main gate, where young men would congregate to share gossip and jokes, like brothers. Whenever a young woman exited the gate by herself, one of the young men would follow her surreptitiously to ensure that she wasn't intercepted by anyone. As soon as she arrived at her destination, the young man guarding her would turn back.

Da'uq did not receive any services from UNRWA, since the area did not lie within its field of operation, so the residents managed by cooperating among themselves to arrange basic services and secure the necessities of life. Electrical lighting, where present, was dim, and the walls of the houses were covered with moss due to the humidity and the water pipes that ran along them. Houses were contiguous, and you could hear the voices of your neighbors having private conversations. The alleys were narrow and intertwining and would not allow two people to pass through side by side. It was a running joke that our parents must have brought the furniture in first and built the house around it. The sewers were visible and only partially covered, serving as a haven for rats and other vermin. When we returned home late at night, we would stomp our feet and sing loudly so as to keep the rats at bay.

The first time I opened my eyes, I would have seen a room containing my parents' bed, a wooden closet with three compartments, and a mountain of mattresses that would be laid down for us at night so that we could sleep side by side. I slept alongside my five brothers and two sisters, pressed close together like sardines in a can. The youngest among us would sleep in a swing consisting of a wooden board covered with bedding, hanging by a rope from the ceiling. Once, my brother Jamal was swinging our youngest brother with considerable force and the swing slammed into the middle door of the closet and smashed it. Jamal was chastised when my mother returned with my father from an evening at the neighbors, but the punishment wasn't as severe as it might have been since my youngest brother was unscathed.

My grandfather and grandmother occupied a room adjacent to ours and they took in each child as he or she reached adolescence. The first to go was my eldest brother, Zuhayr, the darling of my grandmother. He was a well-behaved and calm child and, most importantly, slept early without making a fuss. Next was my brother Muhsin, who annoyed my grandfather because he would stay up all night, moving restlessly and asking endless questions. A kind and patient man, my grandfather was soon at his wits' end. One night when he was trying to find a way to have some private time with my grandmother, he called out to my father: "Ahmad! We were fine with Zuhayr, but not with Muhsin!"

In addition to the two bedrooms, our house had another narrow room serving as a reception area, which was covered by a corrugated tin roof. In winter we listened to the melodious sound of rain on the roof, playing various rhythms and tunes, a symphony that turned menacing when the hail began to fall. In summer, it was transformed into a scorching oven that sent us fleeing to the bedroom or outside to the alleyway. The kitchen, which was also where we bathed, was sectioned off from the reception area. It was a small room dominated by a sink beside a wooden shelf mounted with three gas burners. The surrounding shelves contained numerous pots and pans, and, of course, the indispensable kerosene heater. The toilet was situated right at the entrance of the house, behind a wooden door riddled with holes through which we could see passersby when the main door to the house was open. Because of the tightness of the space no one stayed there long.

My uncle lived in a room on the roof of our house, with the rest of the roof devoted to a clothesline. A large pot in one corner of the roof contained a privet tree with a fragrant aroma that my grandmother adored. To get to the roof, you had to climb two ladders intercepted by a wooden platform. My uncle's room had a bed, a closet with two compartments, and a kerosene heater, and we spent many delightful hours there, especially in wintertime. He would light the kerosene heater, place the top of a tin box over the flame, and roast chestnuts for us. This method, he explained to us, reduced the intensity of the fire so that it didn't scorch the chestnuts and they cooked more evenly. Sometimes he would roast chestnuts, dates, and sweet potatoes together. These moments seem to have happened just yesterday, the taste of chestnuts and dates still lingering on our tongues.

My uncle had a beautiful voice and could play the tabla. He took part in many concerts and often came home tipsy after an alcohol-infused evening. He worked selling vegetables, chickens, and sweets from a pushcart, and I often accompanied him on his rounds during school holidays. He was always happy for me to come along, since I helped him "sell out early," as he often repeated. His customers loved him, especially the women, because of his way with words and his quick wit, and they sometimes came out to see him in their nightgowns.

In one of our rounds before 'Id al-Adha, a woman called out to us from a second-floor window and requested two live chickens. My uncle weighed them and I took them up to her and collected the money. At the end of the day, after "God had bestowed," as my uncle liked to say, we passed by the woman's house again. She called out to my uncle: "Hey, chicken seller, the chickens died! I left them on the roof and they died." It was summer; the sun was blazing and it was scorching hot, so my uncle, with his usual quick wit, replied: "If I'd been left out in this sun I would've burst!" The woman laughed and we joined in before continuing on our way.

My uncle had been stricken with an eye disease in childhood and the condition was exacerbated later in life, weakening his eyesight. I don't know if that had anything to do with the sudden change in his lifestyle that occurred around the same time. He was semiliterate but had memorized the Qur'an by heart, and I remember his transformation from a lover of music and song into a reciter of the Qur'an, a muezzin, and an imam. He never lost his sense of humor, his sociability, and open-mindedness, but he turned into a "modern shaykh" whose resonant voice led him to excel in the recitation of the Qur'an and in performing religious chants.

My uncle married late, which made it necessary for him to move out of his little room on the roof and find a new home. For most of my childhood, the house adjacent to ours was inhabited by a young man and his mother from the town of Shahim in southern Lebanon. His name was Husayn and we just called him Husayn al-Shahimi since we didn't know his last name. When his mother died, he decided to move back to his hometown, and my newly married uncle bought the house and moved into it.

When we were children, the alleyways of Da'uq were our world and our playground. We organized football tournaments and played capture the flag, hopscotch, and an assortment of other games. One of the most important festivals of the year was the commemoration of the Prophet's birth and we would celebrate in the alleys by drawing a circle on the ground in charcoal, dousing it with kerosene, and lighting it up at night along with firecrackers and fireworks.

If childhood was a dream that I lived, adolescence seems like a series of images that I am forever trying to recapture. I try to recall the moments that I entered into the world of adolescence. When the girl next door came of age and grew into her femininity, with her radiant face and shapely figure, feelings of masculinity began to emerge in me and I was constantly trying to catch her attention. I would observe the alley in front of her house and wait for her to emerge to sweep or mop the front steps. If I should be lucky enough to receive a look in my direction, it would unleash in me that sensation that overpowers lovers.

In Da'uq, we always bought our groceries from the shops of resident families. There was the grocery store of Abu 'Adnan and the vegetable store of "al-Shaykh" Sha'ban, who was given that nickname because he would write Qur'anic verses with a brush dipped in ink on the cheeks of children who were afflicted with mumps. There was a widespread belief, which persists, that the swelling would begin to subside as the ink faded and that it would vanish entirely once the ink had disappeared. There was also the pickle store of Abu Ahmad Asraf and the cake bakery of the Abu Qaba' family, where we could buy pieces of leftover cake for a pittance. There was a tailor shop, owned by Anis al-'Umari, who specialized in shirts, and a butcher shop owned by al-Hajj "al-Kak," at least that was his nickname. There was even Abu Husah's, a store dedicated to slicing and washing carrots, apples, and other fruit, to be sent to a juice shop outside the neighborhood.

Our greatest delight was reserved for the traveling candy salesman, Naji, who was at least sixty years old, a tall man with long gray hair and deeply lined cheeks. He always wore a heavy coat even in the height of summer, trousers with rolled-up cuffs, and tattered shoes. He pushed a worn-out children's stroller filled with an assortment of candy, chocolates, and multicolored balloons, as well as some miscellaneous toys. Naji was generous to a fault, giving children who had no money whatever they wanted for free. The thing that amazed me most was that he would give children a plastic pistol and ask them to aim at a target like a clothesline on a nearby roof, and when they fired he would cry out: "Boooom! Bravo! You hit it!" The clothesline or other target would not have moved, but he still gave the child a gift in reward for good marksmanship. I never knew whether he was having fun at the children's expense or whether all he wanted was to make us happy.

Naji had a university degree and spoke several languages. People used to make fun of him and say that too much education, reading, and knowledge had driven him to madness, for that was the widespread belief. After Naji went missing for a long time, we learned that he had passed away. With his passing, the smiles that he had left on children's faces also disappeared, which raises the question: who was the real lunatic?

The inhabitants of Da'uq lived as one family in many houses, and in the month of Ramadan we became one large household. The variety of dishes served at mealtimes multiplied and neighbors exchanged platters of food and dessert. In the final week of Ramadan, the little shops teemed with semolina, nuts, dates, and shortening of all kinds. The women would congregate every evening to prepare ma'mul and ka'k pastries for the celebration of 'Id al-Fitr. They met in a different house each evening until they had prepared enough pastries for everyone. My great-aunt on my mother's side, "*Sitti*" Hajjeh Umm 'Ali, was always present at these evening gatherings and was the most active and enthusiastic when it came to preparing the pastries. The role of myself and other youngsters was to carry the large round aluminum pans containing the pastries to one of the two bakeries. We would balance them on our heads and take them to either Ahmad al-Hajj's bakery or that of Abu Hattah. The baking would be done in the predawn hours and the caravans carrying the pastries would return home in the early morning.

On the eve of 'Id al-Fitr, Sabra Square became a beehive of activity, a busy marketplace for butchers to sell their meat and chicken. Cages full of chickens were stacked on top of one another, and the butchers would stand behind their scales, poised to weigh the chicken selected by the customer. After it was weighed, it was slaughtered and then caught by a boy standing by a pot of boiling water, who would scald it before throwing it into a chicken plucker, a kind of rotating barrel with protrusions like little rubber fingers. The chicken would emerge plucked of all of its feathers, it would be rinsed in water, and then presented to the customer.

Butchers, who stayed up all night, constructed makeshift stables around their shops in which they kept their sheep and cows, tethered by ropes, or held in by wooden boards. If you wandered around Da'uq at night you would be greeted by the hum of the glowing kerosene heaters, upon which the 'Id meal was prepared. You would take in the fragrant aromas of meat, chicken, and rice pilaf covered with nuts. You would hear mothers urging their children to hurry up and bathe so that they would be ready in the morning to wear their new 'Id clothes.

Before the dawn call to prayer, the men would head off to the mosque accompanied by their sons to perform the 'Id prayer, wearing their traditional dishdasha gowns and white skullcaps, which were brought back each year by pilgrims returning from Mecca. On their way back from the mosque they passed by the coffeehouses and pastry sellers to buy kanafeh pastries for breakfast. In our excitement over the 'Id and our new clothes, we would wake up early to greet the feast. I can still remember the morning of the 'Id when I went over to visit "*Sitti*" Umm 'Ali, my maternal great-aunt, after she had become partially paralyzed and was unable to stand up. When I knocked on her door carrying a gift of oranges, her husband opened it. She was lying in her bed with her head resting on the headboard. She looked at me with tears in her eyes, having never had children of her own. I strode toward her with a smile, saying: "May each year bring you happiness." As soon as I was close enough she hurried to clasp me to her breast so that I could embrace her. Her white nightgown gave off a fragrant scent. She kissed me, taking deep breaths from my neck, and then insisted on offering me some sweets and a holiday gift of money, over my protests. She told me that I had done what none of the adults had done by visiting her. Later, when she succumbed to disease and passed away, everyone missed her and cried over her. The women still remember her fondly whenever they get together, especially at the time of the 'Id feast. May "*Sitti*" Umm 'Ali rest in peace.

We still have close ties to some of the families that we lived and grew up with. And though we've lost touch with others, their names remain carved in our memories: Shakatna, Ahwal, Sirri, Ghazalah, Maraqah, Jajah, Iskandarani, Sa'di, Sawwan, Irwadi, Qambur, Sahli, Yasin, Huwaylu, Mughayyir, Abu 'Adas, Hallaq, Abu Qaba', Khazandar, Buhayri, Minawi, Yasir, Sirhan, Far, Maslakhawi, 'Ayyash, Handam, Kasita, Sadiq, Ghaban, Ghabayin, Asraf, Bushnaq, Shafi'I, Kabbarah, Ghazzawi, Lahham, Zaydan, Hafi, Abu Shanab, Dababish, Sa'idi, Sundus, Zaydan, Safadi, Za'inni, Zughbi, 'Uways, Hindawi, Mashharawi, 'Abdul Rahim, Abu 'Afash, Na'na', all of them families from the towns and villages of Palestine.

In 1969, my mother suffered from a swelling in her head that had to be surgically removed, as a result of which she lost her memory. That same year, I lost my grandfather on my father's side, who was a mentor to me and my greatest advocate. I used to read him stories of 'Antar bin Shaddad and the womanizer Salem Abu Layla al-Muhalhal, and he was the person who turned me into a storyteller, encouraged my love of reading, and broadened my imaginative horizons.

My grandfather worked as a used clothes salesman in downtown Beirut. He partnered with a Lebanese friend of his whom he had met when the latter would visit Jaffa for business before it was occupied. My grandfather used to spend most of the day at work, returning in the afternoon carrying a leather suitcase, which was more like a large bag, packed with fruits and vegetables. His pockets would always be weighed down with candies, which he doled out to the children of the family and the whole neighborhood. We thronged to welcome him as soon as he entered the alley-way, chanting: "Kids! Jiddu is here!" He would repeat the chant after us with indescribable joy and an ever-present smile, despite his weariness from standing on his feet for hours. Then he would spread his arms to embrace us and march us home.

My grandfather, may he rest in peace, told me stories about when I was very young, among them certain grown-up fears and premonitions. In 1958, the year after I was born, during the crisis in Lebanon that was called a "revolution," my great-aunt was visiting our house and, before she sat down, she asked my one-year-old self: "What's the news?" "Ta-boooom," was my reply, and she fled immediately, because as soon as I said it, we heard the sound of gun-fire and armed skirmishes. Many times that year, my father returned from work on his hands and knees.

My parents were like lovebirds. The passion between Ahmad and Fatima was beyond words. He used to call her "piece of chocolate" because of her brown skin, and on weekends they wore matching clothes. My father's jacket, shirt, and trousers were matched with my mother's suit, or shirt and skirt. Even his shoes, her shoes, and her handbag were color-coordinated. He stood tall at 195 centimeters, whereas she passed on to me her shortness of stature. All eyes would be on them as they traversed the alley to visit the

'Arus al-Bahr Café in Beirut, or the Bardawni Restaurant in Zahleh. But my father also took an interest in us children and we went out together for many enjoyable excursions. Many evenings he returned late from work with delicious treats, grilled meats, pastries, or fruits, and would ask my mother to wake us up to share them, not heeding her protests that it was too late. In those moments, he just wanted to be surrounded by us.

Before my mother became ill, my father dedicated his life to work, night and day, in order to secure the family's livelihood. Her illness devastated him and he sought refuge in alcohol, trying to forget the tragedy that had befallen him at the age of thirty-five. He had been deprived of the pleasure of life with his soul mate. One day, he returned at dawn in a drunken state to the apartment he had rented for my mother after her operation, when the doctors had recommended she be housed in a specially equipped residence. That day, my brother Muhsin was on duty with my mother and he greeted my father by saying: "What are you doing to yourself and to us? Is this what my mother would have done if something similar had happened to you, God forbid?" Muhsin cried and so did my father. Then he went to the bathroom and washed himself as though he were cleansing himself of a sin he had committed. After that, he hugged my brother and promised never to do it again, and he never did.

My father was a single parent to six boys, two girls, and a wife who was more like a newborn child. She lived among us though she didn't know us and we meant nothing to her. She received treatment in the form of electric-shock therapy twice a week. We would observe her closely, looking at her intently, and it would bring us to tears, but we never once gave up hope that she would return to us, as long as she lived among us.

My father was unable to manage the affairs of his family, since he had spent most of his life working long hours to secure life's necessities for his large brood. My mother had been the one responsible for our care and upbringing, and for all matters of the household. My two older brothers, Zuhayr and Muhsin, like many young men, spent most of their time outside the house. When they returned late at night, they would climb the wall of our neighbors' house and jump onto our roof. Then they would slip into my uncle's room, who would cover for them by saying that they had stayed up with him for the night. I was in the middle of the pack, shy to the point of seclusion, afraid of mixing with people, and diffident. I was always charged with caring for my younger brother Jamal, since he suffered from rheumatism, which affected his heart and caused us all great distress as a result. He was forbidden from all sports and was not supposed to exert any physical effort. Most doctors thought it was not advisable to operate on him at that time, but they warned us that he would need surgery in the future and, sure enough, six years ago he was given an artificial heart-valve replacement. Jamal was obsessed with football and I would have to reluctantly deny his pleas to join his friends when they played. Incapable of resisting his wishes for long, I sometimes relented and allowed him to play for a short time. The next day, he would wake up unwell, with swollen feet, and I would be punished for being remiss in caring for him.

To compensate us for the loss of maternal affection, my father started spending more time with us. We would stay up with him in the evenings, and he would tell us about his true love, Jaffa. He told us stories of his life in the city and the hardships he endured in childhood. When he was merely a boy, he was sent to work in a restaurant serving ful, leaving home in the early dawn and returning in the afternoon. The alleys of Jaffa knew him well, since he would stroll along them throughout the night until daybreak. In those days, people told tales of the jinn, stories that terrified a boy who walked the streets of the old city at night. He told us about the haunted well and the abandoned house, and about the female jinn who appeared to him one day, sending him running in fright while muttering verses from the Qur'an.

One evening, he told us a story that may have been the product of his imagination, or an allegory he had heard from others, or a result of what he saw when he made deliveries from the restaurant to the houses of "ladies of the evening" at dawn. He related: "A young man wanted to get married and sought his father's advice. His father told him that if he wanted to marry, he should seek out his bride in the early morning as soon she woke up. He would then see her true beauty unadorned with cosmetics."

My older sister Bakiza took over the tasks of cooking, washing, caring for the little ones, and household chores. I was happy to help her out. When one of my cousins, who lived in Kuwait, asked for her hand in marriage, it was as though destiny was putting me on trial, testing my ability to take on responsibility. It had barely been two years since my mother's affliction. At first, my father opposed the marriage, but after relatives intervened, and upon considering the struggles that my sister had endured, he agreed to a one-year engagement followed by marriage. My mother had prepared the bridal trousseau of her younger sisters, but she couldn't do the same for her own daughter; my cousin prepared my sister's trousseau.

The day that Bakiza left to join her husband was a difficult one. My sister hugged me and we squeezed each other very tightly. She was the closest of my siblings to me, a true partner in mind and spirit. She held me in her eyes as if to say: "I know that it's a large and demanding responsibility, my brother, but it's up to you to take care of the family, and I'm sure that you'll rise to the challenge." Fortunately, I had learned a lot from her.

My challenging journey began with meal preparation, which was something that baffled me. For my first attempt at making rice, the measurements were all off and the result was a kind of rice pudding, but everyone had to eat it anyway. Afterward, I had some cooking sessions with my grandmother, who taught me all the measurements, and eventually the family ate their meals with greater confidence and satisfaction.

We left Da'uq during the armed conflict between the Palestinian resistance forces and the Lebanese army in 1973. We sought refuge with friends before moving to the quarter of al-Basta al-Fawqa, which was near to where my mother was being treated.

Our dire circumstances did not prevent us from pursuing our education. I was always near the top of my class and my artistic talent grew with time. I studied at the Ya'bad school for girls and boys, run by UNRWA in the Dana neighborhood. One day in the fourth grade, I was bent over my desk, focused on a drawing of a multicolored bird, and I didn't notice the teacher standing over me. I only became aware of her presence when she stopped explaining the lesson and fell silent—I raised my head to find her right there in front of me. She looked at me and said: "Finish the drawing and give it to me." She didn't punish me because I excelled in my studies. That was a kind gesture on the part of my beloved teacher, Lutfiyah Sakhnini, whose glowing and beautiful features I still remember well.

I left school after the intermediate or middle school stage. Like many others of my generation, I was swept up in the turmoil of political, ideological, and social transformations, as well as the successive armed conflicts. I found myself caught in both private and public struggles. I had never been religious but as a child I prayed and fasted, just as my parents had done. As I got older, I experienced personal strife and entertained a series of different convictions. I never became an atheist, but I did relinquish prayer and fasting. I had a succession of occupations and found employment as a carpenter, painter, and photographer, as well as at a printing press, a journalistic institution, and a research center. I am married with a family and have become a grandfather.

My mother eventually regained some of her memory, and it was as though she had returned from the past. She was able to recall more distant memories but had trouble with more recent ones. With time, her children had grown up and married, and they rejoiced in having her back among them, joking with her grandchildren and telling them whatever stories she managed to remember. But, as though to deprive us of our joy, destiny played a cruel trick on us. My brother Muhsin, a husband and father of two young children, went to work on the morning of October 14, 1988, with his five-year-old son Shadi trailing after him. "Baba," his son called out to him, "are you coming back today?" "Of course, I'm coming back," Muhsin replied. But he didn't come back that day, since he died a martyr in a massive explosion that killed many people in the Dana neighborhood. My uncle and I both set off to break the news to my mother. My uncle arrived first, having taken the mission upon himself, and I followed him within minutes. I found him sitting beside her while she cried. "Mother," I said, "God did not want him to suffer, so he relieved him of suffering." The news hit her like a thunderbolt and she sprang up crying, "He diiiiiied!" She ran out of the house in her house clothes with her head bare. My uncle had not dared tell her that Muhsin had died and had instead said that he was in hospital. What had I done to my poor mother?

The news came as a violent shock to my mother, and acted as a jolt to her brain, which had defied all treatment. Suddenly, it seemed as though her memory was completely restored.

In 2005, though, our journey of suffering continued; it sometimes seemed as though we were a magnet for hardship. My mother had a stroke that paralyzed her and made her lose the power of speech. We had to mash up her food and pass it through a feeding tube that went from her nose to her stomach. Even medicine had to be ground up to pass through the tube. It was excruciatingly difficult to lose her in this way, bit by bit. She had once been the center of our lives and we were now powerless to alleviate her pain and agony. Finally, she seemed to want to relieve us from the suffering and put an end to the tragedy. My mother died.

My father, Fatima's lover, never drank coffee or ate food when offering his condolences to her friends and relatives, perhaps for fear of death or in awe of the momentous event. After my mother's burial he asked me to bring him her mattress and set it on his bed for him to sleep on. He said to me: "Her mattress is tender, son." We used to eavesdrop at his bedroom door, listening to him singing songs with familiar tunes whose lyrics he had rewritten for my mother. Later I learned that he had recorded these songs on tapes, which my brother found in his bedside table. The story of Fatima and Ahmad lives on, and we can tell it to our children and grandchildren. Their love story is cited by everyone who knew them. For some, it's seen as a revival of the classic tale of Qays and Layla, because of my father's intense loyalty, devotion, and attachment to her in life, illness, and even after her death.

My father wanted his death to be the end of his misfortunes. He died crossing the street with my younger brother Sa'd as they went to offer their condolences for the death of a relative. A motorcycle driver ran into my father at an insane speed. He was thrown several meters into the air and fell on his head, shattering his skull. The last time I saw my father was the evening before the accident, when I visited him on Father's Day. I will never forget that evening. My brothers were teasing him and talking about my mother, whose picture was in front of him. He pointed to the picture and talked to it: "That's enough, I'm coming to join you." He had made a rendezvous with her.

My uncle was imam and muezzin of the Salah al-Din mosque into his old age, and he would head off there every morning, leaning on his cane. The mosque was only meters from his home. Even after his death, they still broadcast a recording of the adhan in his voice from the minaret five times a day, to honor his memory and his voice. My brother Muhsin, the "Don Juan" of the neighborhood, passed away without being able to share in the joys of his children's weddings or relish the sight of his grandchildren. We also miss my brother Khalid, the seventh child, with his ready smile, good-natured character, and simplicity. The alleys that he played in grieve for him. He succumbed to a muscular disease and, after fighting it for two years, passed away last year.

I stand today before the main entrance to Da'uq to find that it is no longer as it was. Gone is Abu Muhammad and the sound of Umm Kulthum. Gone is Subhi al-Batal. All those faces have disappeared. Many young people left their families in Da'uq for a new diaspora, after the series of tumultuous events that unfolded there. There were the battles between the Lebanese army and Palestinian resistance forces in 1973, followed by the Lebanese civil war in 1975–1976, the Israeli invasion of Lebanon in 1982, and the Sabra and Shatila massacre. The perpetrators of the massacre entered Da'uq from the direction of Gaza Hospital and called on people to come forward. My brother-in-law was one of them, but he escaped in the direction of Dana station and managed to save his life.

The most difficult and painful events were those associated with the War of the Camps in 1985, which pitted the Amal Movement against the Palestinian resistance. Da'uq was besieged and houses were destroyed on top of their inhabitants. Many people were killed, and the stories told by former residents sound like figments of the imagination. They tell of a small area whose narrow alleyways could hardly hold its inhabitants before it was destroyed, transformed into a mound of rubble covering human remains. A man called Abu

'Abd left his mother behind because she was semi-paralyzed and immobile. She said to him: "Son, I have a feeling that the end is near. You've tried to lift me and you couldn't. You won't be able to carry me away from here. Get away while you can. I don't want to cause you any inconvenience or be the cause of your family losing you. They're out already and they have a greater right to you. They're the future. Go, my son, may God be content with you. There's life and then there's the afterlife. Just leave the water bottle next to me with the last loaf of bread. I don't even know if I can finish it. Go, my son, and don't look back." Abu 'Abd crawled out through the debris, found his family and embraced them, and cried like a child. When he later returned, and the debris had been removed, he cradled his mother's body. They had bulldozed the rubble, which was mixed in with furniture, valuable possessions, and the human remains of the martyrs.

A man named Bilal had stayed alone in Da'uq once the siege began, after his family had been evacuated to a safe area. Hours before the militias entered the ruins of Da'uq, shooting in all directions in search of fighters, Bilal escaped to a house adjacent to Da'uq belonging to a friendly Lebanese family. They hid him in the attic of their house in anticipation of a door-to-door search. Soon enough, an armed group from the Amal Movement forced their way into the house in search of those who had fled from their infernal fire. Bilal was infuriated because of his concern for the family that had taken him in. His ammunition had run out; he was powerless and he bit his finger so hard that he cut off a piece without feeling any pain. Today, Bilal is in Denmark.

The alleys and passageways of Da'uq are no longer a playground for memories and longing. The houses that now stand in Da'uq, rebuilt after a long struggle with the authorities to get materials in, are not the same, nor are their inhabitants. There are open areas that were never there before. Some faces have vanished and others have replaced them. I search in vain for my father, worshipping at the shrine of my mother.

New shops have opened, selling new varieties of fruits and exotic foods, after many migrant workers from Bangladesh and Sri Lanka settled in the vicinity of Da'uq. The Islamic Seniors' Home, that "safe haven," is still there. We used to talk to the residents when we were little and were entertained by the beautiful singing voices wafting out of its windows. In the evenings, we were sometimes frightened by the cries of pain. During the Israeli invasion, many artillery shells fell in the perimeter of the building and all the patients, nurses, and administrators were crowded into the ground floor, which resembled a dark tunnel. The administration of the Seniors' Home issued a call to all those who had relatives there asking them to evacuate them quickly, as they could no longer ensure their safety or take responsibility for keeping them there under bombardment. My wife's brother's mother-in-law worked at the Seniors' Home, so my brother-in-law and I set off together from our house in the Basta neighborhood without telling our families, under cover of night. We managed to flag down a passing truck belonging to the Palestinian resistance, which we took all the way to the Dana neighborhood. There was destruction everywhere. An outpost belonging to the Palestinian Armed Struggle had been decimated by Israeli aircraft machine guns, which made the plot of land around it look like a plowed agricultural field. The sky was lit up with incandescent flares.

There were fires blazing in homes on both sides of the road from Dana to Sabra Square. The buildings surrounding the Seniors' Home were ablaze. My brother-in-law and I entered the tunnel-like hallway where everyone in the building had sought refuge. A man in his seventies sprang up in front of me in his blue undergarments. His face was pale and his hair disheveled, and he cried: "Where are we going to sleep?" I sidestepped him only to be accosted by an eighty-year-old woman, who held onto my arm and implored me: "Take me with you." Even though I had just dodged missiles and fire without fear, I couldn't take any more and felt utterly powerless. What could I offer them? What form of protection could I provide when all the humanitarian and international organizations had failed? My brother-in-law called out to me: "Where to now?" I wanted to go outside. Standing outside in the open air under the shelling was easier for me than standing powerless before those poor wretches.

The Seniors' Home has now expanded but its windows are still covered by screens, behind which shadows dance, some of them belonging to residents who have been there all along and others to new arrivals. The residents shout, sing, cry, call out in pain, and wave their arms as though no years have passed and as if time was still expecting their return to someplace. A return to a homeland that lives inside us in our diaspora, wherever we are.

I offer my apologies to all those people in Da'uq with whom I spent my life and whom I have not mentioned, and to all the shopkeepers whose shops I was happy to frequent, but whose memories I have not recalled. They are all in my heart and mind and I hope to be reunited with them on the soil of our beloved Palestine upon our return.

Shorter and Longer than a Winter's Cold Spell

YAFA TALAL EL-MASRI

(b. Beirut, 1990)

Your memory is everything, your only weapon. Without a recording device, you're at the mercy of time. You approach the edge of the cliff without so much as a safety net.

Everything in life is momentary. We're all honest and we all mean what we say—in that moment alone. There's no such thing as lying, there are just some things that are true for a very short period of time. Things that are true in a specific place and time, that's all.

A man has no duplicity in him when he tells a woman he loves her. Between her skin and his sweat, a wine-drenched, gorgeous passion emerges, and when his feet hit the marble floor, that passion dies a martyr's death. He didn't lie to her at all, but passion's lifespan is exceedingly short. It can be measured by the better part of a night or longer, or the layer of frost on a tent. But passion, my dear, however much it alters, remains passion; no other name fits it. And the same goes for love of the homeland.

We all mean what we say when we tell a lie. And we've all traded a noble cause for a brief period of happiness, whether it lasted moments, or days, or even years.

"We will never in our lifetimes know how much exactly they sold Palestine for," my grandfather always said, though I never met him.

They sold it without anyone recording anything at all. Nobody wrote about their feelings when they took one last look at their houses. No one made a record for me of the appearance of the tiled roof of our house in Jaffa, or of the names of the flowers that grew in our garden.

Here, I'm going to simply record everything I've felt, even if those feelings only lasted for a few moments. Don't short-lived things also deserve to be celebrated? Doesn't exile deserve to be spoken of?

My Short-Lived Lie

I'm going to confess something to you. I remember my childhood well, even those details that my parents think I don't remember. I remember the whole story from the beginning. It began when my father, a patriotic fighter in the ranks of the Popular Front, named me after his birthplace, "Yafa" (Jaffa).

He called me "Yafa" simply because Palestinian refugees assume many habits that are beyond their control, notably the tendency to reopen old wounds with their nails each day to prevent them from healing. It's an entrenched habit and there's no use trying to convince a refugee to refrain. Like all those who left Palestine as children, my father wanted to shout out his hometown's name every morning, and he wanted his hometown to respond with a smile.

When I was born, my four brothers were already young men. They gathered around and the eldest one said: "Did you just now give us a sister? She hasn't even arrived in time to iron our shirts." He was right: I had barely begun my journey by the time they had moved on to another exile.

I grew up in Burj al-Barajneh, south of Beirut. For "Yafa" to live in "Beirut" is a kind of struggle in its own right. I began to understand this struggle when I turned sixteen, after which, for the next ten years, I didn't age a single season. Every night in bed, I would hug a stuffed bear and recount what I saw in the camp that morning. I would tell him stories about a child whose idea of beauty went no further than her own braids, who happily swam through the muddy alleyways of the camp. And about another child who devoured ice cream voraciously, after tasting it for the first time.

After my ten-year period of seclusion, in which I remained a prisoner of adolescence, I decided to follow the herd again and I proceeded to age ten years each year. Maybe I was trying to make up for lost time, or maybe I was preparing to live a short life and save myself from wrinkles, bitterness, and memories, or the absence thereof.

I indulge in all kinds of risk and recklessness. There are many things I need to experience in the short life that I've been granted—a life that seems no longer than a winter's cold spell. I engage in all types of deception. I take on a different personality in a dark costume that I wear in spite of myself, in an office that puts me in a box. I try to advance professionally with false ambition. However, as a refugee, I need to evade the Lebanese labor laws that prevent me from pursuing my profession. But my name always betrays me and exposes the deception.

How unjust are the laws that transform our love for our homeland into shame. And how ashamed I am to think that one day my father may read about what the name he chose for me has caused, and what the blue-colored travel document I inherited from him has wrought.

The Dream that Could Ignite a Civil War

Like every girl, I dreamed since childhood about my wedding day.

I didn't do so in my zeal to silence the women of the camp who were plagued by "spinster-phobia," nor because the idea of marriage seemed romantic. My interest was purely in the wedding itself. I was always planning the day in my head. I wanted it to be a traditional Palestinian wedding, with a hand-embroidered *'abaya* instead of a white dress. And, maybe, instead of a veil, I would wear a kufiyah attached carefully with two braids of hair. We wouldn't listen to any of the singers from the television or radio; we would sway in style to the songs of Palestinian villages taught to daughters by their mothers.

> *Tell his mother to rejoice and celebrate*
>
> *And sprinkle the pillows with perfume and scent,*
>
> *The home is blessed and the house is built,*
>
> *The party is ours and the couple will prosper.*

I was no more than ten years old when I hatched the grand plan for my wedding.

Since weddings in Palestine are usually celebrated in town squares, and there was no suitable square in Beirut, my imagination settled on the one place that would serve the purpose. It was a spot my father often took us: the main square in the town of Dayr al-Qamar.

Being raised by an Arabic teacher and a former militant in the Popular Front has some inevitable consequences. For one thing, you're exposed to many lectures about history and language from an early age. And you hear many unique stories about the struggle that you would never come across in a documentary film or read in a journalist's report. On our spring and summer outings, every single time we passed through Dayr al-Qamar we would be regaled with the same lecture.

My father would tell us that it was once the capital of the Ma'ni princes of Lebanon, that it was an archetypal Christian town with six famous churches, and that in the middle of the town there was a mosque built by Fakhr al-Din the First.

The main square in Dayr al-Qamar always cast a spell on me. I would sit alongside my parents at the edge of the square in the evening while they admired its proximity to the sky and observed the way it embraced nightfall. They watched the water pouring playfully out of the fountain. Meanwhile, I would picture myself in a red-and-white *thawb* from Jaffa while a hundred young men and women danced the *dabkeh* around me, twirling their kufiyahs to a tune playing loudly in my head.

> *You're tall and cute, let me tell you something,*
> *You're going away but your homeland is better!*
> *I'm afraid, my dears, that he'll settle down,*
> *Befriending others and forgetting me.*

The town square in Dayr al-Qamar was my only choice for a wedding location and I wouldn't settle for anything else. It virtually exuded tradition, with its cool water fountain that quenched the summer heat, its arches and its stage, the stones that had witnessed eons of history, and the trees that ringed the monastery and welcomed you into their shade. I had no inkling of Lebanese politics at that time and therefore no idea that the realization of my dream would have ignited a civil war.

I was completely unaware then of the magnitude of civil sensitivities that decades of war had burdened us with.

On one of our trips, we stopped at the town square as usual and carried our plastic water jugs to fill up at the fountain. I pointed to three commemorative plaques in the square and asked my father about them. He explained that the first honored the restoration of the square, the second was in memory of assassinated leader Dany Chamoun, and the third marked the end of renovations in 1991.

Even though my father would have liked to narrate the entire history of the world if time allowed, he avoided telling me about Dany Chamoun and the war in the mountains of Lebanon. But the histories of wars are contained in thousands of books and old newspapers, even if no one wants to talk about them.

That day, everything changed. I understood for the first time what it meant to live in a nation devoured by civil war, extinguishing every last smile. Dayr al-Qamar, whose sight was always a pleasure for me, which I was instinctively attached to, was once attacked by the Palestinians during the war of the mountains.

I hadn't known that a single kufiyah could lead to a sea of blood. I hadn't known the depths of hatred we generated and inherited. Even our celebrations could aggravate others, and their aggravation could be a cause for our celebration. Dear friends, it was just a child's dream.

That day, I understood the meaning of politics for the first time. Politics had killed the small child that lived inside me for a little longer than she should have.

I don't blame the disruption of my dream on politics alone. There was another problem, an important detail that my fantasy omitted. I completely forgot that the wedding would require a partner who was willing to put up with my childish naivete and replace his suit with a kufiyah and baggy pants. The possibility of finding such a man was a mission no less difficult than liberation of the land, a task more arduous than celebrating a Palestinian wedding in Dayr al-Qamar.

But to this day, when I pass through the main square in Dayr al-Qamar, I allow myself to fantasize about songs among the stones of the Ma'ni princes. Nothing can dissuade me from imagining, since imagination is free and the wedding will never happen anyway.

Living in the Republic of Fingers

Dear reader, if you're well versed in politics, then you're no doubt consumed by laughter right now, amused by the naivete of my dream. We're all funny in childhood, carefree in our habits and fantasies that transcend the boring realities of maturity. Many of us name things as children. We assign names to dolls and objects and sometimes those names stick over time. Nasri, however, named his fingers.

I would see Nasri every time we visited relatives in Tripoli and he aroused my curiosity more than all the young men in Beirut. Nasri lived in Nahr al-Barid camp, situated along the sea. As I remember it, the camp was always sunny, and on each visit, Nasri's smile eclipsed the sun.

Nasri didn't call me by a special nickname, as my other friends did, but he had very special names for his fingers. The names weren't random but were carefully chosen, like the names of eagerly awaited newborn children that are dutifully recorded on food ration cards. He started inevitably with his thumbs, which represented our gateway to Palestine, calling them "Ramallah." From there we proceed, stealthily, to the rest: the pointer finger he called "Jerusalem," the middle finger was "Abu Mazin," the next was "Struggle," and the pinky "Return."

The rest of us used our fingers to count our remaining vacation days and the coins in our pocket, checking to see if we had enough to buy a supply of candy. But Nasri used the fingers of his right hand to count the number of newborns in Nahr al-Barid who were given the names of Palestinian towns. He would repeatedly measure the distance between Return and Jerusalem. Sometimes he found himself in a real predicament; for example, when the West Bank rose up in anger, he found that Struggle gravitated toward Ramallah instead of lining up with the other fingers. At other times, he would look at his fingers and bend them so as to try to separate Struggle from Abu Mazin as much as he could, just so that everything was spaced logically. But his hand remained a single unit despite his efforts. Anyway, how could the one in the middle let the other fingers fight on their own?

I have already confided in you my secret ignorance of politics. I was never able to follow Nasri's discussions of the dialectic between truth and falsehood. I couldn't keep up with his attempts to intervene in the conflicts between the five digits, for governing the Republic of Fingers is far more difficult than you might imagine.

For a long time, I wasn't sure that I wanted to be a citizen in the Republic of Fingers; it seemed crowded enough with its five residents.

In 2008, when we were in secondary school, the battle of the camp of Nahr al-Barid broke out in northern Lebanon, where Nasri and his fingers resided. Nasri, who would always say that the Nahr (River) neighborhood where he lived was the most beautiful and calmest neighborhood in the camp, found himself occupied with pulling bodies out of the river. When he found them, they had usually been lying there for several days, for fallen martyrs are also calm.

From that time onward, caught between those who justified a second Palestinian Nakba and those who claimed to know what really happened in the camp, I sank ever deeper into the gap that separated Lebanese citizens and the Palestinian refugees who had lived in Lebanon temporarily for sixty-eight years. I checked my principles at the door and walked alongside everyone else down the alley of prejudice.

Nasri, meanwhile, lost everything but his principles. The battle of the camp did not just cost him his memories of before, it also cost him his house in the Nahr neighborhood, four friends in the massacre of the bread truck, and one of his fingers.

On one of the last nights of the battle, Nasri, alongside many other camp residents who had been unable to leave, decided to seek refuge in a shelter at the Samed community center. As shelling intensified from the warships offshore and rained down on the community center, all the surrendered souls perished in silence.

Nasri didn't die but he witnessed the death of everyone else.

He emerged with a hand wound and they had to amputate Ramallah.

Any human being would be psychologically and physically traumatized by the amputation of a finger, so you can imagine the effect on an extraordinary young man who used to name his fingers. It seemed to me that Nasri had lost a son of his own flesh and blood, in addition to the homeland that he often dreamt of seeing.

On my first visit after the battle, I didn't go with a bouquet of roses; that wasn't Nasri's style. He would have been happier with a dozen falafel or a new music album. I went carrying Murid Barghouti's novel, *I Saw Ramallah*. His prominent teeth gleamed when he saw it in my hand. He reached out his four remaining fingers and motioned excitedly for me to hand him the book.

He caressed the book's cover with his Republic of Fingers, now missing one member, and flipped the pages quickly until he settled on a random sentence that was chosen for him by Return. He read it out:

"Our people, who moved out of necessity from one part of the homeland to another, and took up residence in our mountainous towns and villages, we called them refugees! We called them migrants! Who will apologize to them? Who will apologize to us? Who will explain to whom this great confusion?"

He read it with bated breath like someone wrestling with fear under gunfire. Then he raised his face slowly and wearily to meet my glistening eyes, and said with a smile: "I wish they'd taken Abu Mazin and left Ramallah."

The Prick of a Needle

We lost contact with Nasri for several years; he disappeared into a mystical trance while he tried to forgive himself. Then, on my twenty-second birthday, Nasri emerged from his hermitage to make an appearance at my raucous party, bringing a gift of a kufiyah.

It was no ordinary kufiyah; it had been brought by a friend from Ramallah to Beirut. When she found out that it was to be a birthday present, she said: "Really, Nasri? You're going to give her a kufiyah? What kind of a present is that?"

Our friend, whom we envied for living in Palestine, didn't understand the value of earth and threads from Palestine for a refugee who thought that Palestine was a myth. She never understood why we hugged her at such length whenever she came to visit. She was never convinced that the air felt and smelled differently in Palestine and Lebanon, or rather, in Palestine and the rest of the world.

I unfolded and spread out the kufiyah, as Nasri's eyes met mine, waiting expectantly for my surprise to be reflected in my facial features. As I draped it across my lap, I noticed that it was teeming with unusual embroidery, like the pattern found on a thawb. It reminded me of the embroidered wedding dress that I had folded and stashed away in the closet of my dreams. I ran my fingers gently along the edges of the kufiyah as my mind played the screenplay for my pre-wedding arrangements. I would put the final touches on the kohl around my eyes and slowly attach my bridal veil with a pin. The pin would lightly prick my finger and the drops of blood would stain my white dress . . .

Just a minute . . . what's this blood? The veil was just a daydream, but the pain was real and so were the drops of blood on my hand—where had they come from? I had pricked my finger on a real needle that had broken off and been left in the kufiyah by the tailor who had worked on it.

I held the needle in a daze, suddenly forgetting time and space, and noticed that between the broken needle and the thread were clustered a few fine hairs. I forgot all about Nasri, who was waiting expectantly for my reaction to his gift. My head was filled with a multitude of images. This needle had been used by a lady in Palestine to sew hundreds of kufiyahs, and this one was the most important of them all. That was her hair and this cluster testified to the sweat of her brow. As she worked, the hairs had got tangled between the thread and the needle.

This lady has long black hair and I hope she has the time to comb it every day and let it hang over her shoulders, without a scarf on her head. I think she has dark skin and I'm sure she's extremely beautiful. I imagine she's in her thirties, she learned embroidery at an early age from her grandmother, and she lives in Umm al-Sharayit in Ramallah. At least, I'd like to live in that neighborhood. I would describe her house, but I don't know what houses in Palestine look like; I don't know how people walk in the streets, nor how people talk there. I'm reluctant to misdescribe things and provoke ridicule.

Dear lady, I don't know who you are, and I don't know if you left a strand of your hair and your needle on purpose, or whether you did so accidentally because you were engrossed in your work. But whoever you are, you've awakened my dream.

Your simple act may have been the reason for my leaving Beirut to find a hidden part of myself. Or maybe I had many other reasons, but your strand of hair is the one I remember because it was the straw that broke the camel's back. And maybe that camel was the one that carried my grandmother from her village, al-Kabri, in northern Palestine to Lebanon.

I don't know if Nasri, the main source of all this madness, will consent to leaving with me. He might just prefer to stay near his new camp, guarding its indigenous inhabitants from the colonial powers that were on this land before him. It doesn't matter. I might start a series of investigations, a search mission for you that will take me to Palestine. You might just be my excuse to travel to Palestine. I may find you there, at the margin, or I might draw the margin and find myself where I always thought I would.

A Small House in Canada

Margins, lines, white sheets of paper. That is how the noisy interference started in my head. I was filled with questions about the point of my existence in exile, and my head teemed with thoughts of the covert enmity between Palestinians and Lebanese. I withdrew from the society that was hosting us, confined to a box that shuttled between home, the camp, and the UNRWA school. I barely saw anyone but Palestinians in Lebanon, even as the Lebanese population passed close to me every day.

As a result of being confined to that box, if you had stripped me naked, you would have found that I was wearing torn socks and that I stank of the camp that I inhabited in their nightmares. As for the point of a life of refuge, that was a puzzle for which the only solution I could find was to leave, to abandon refuge for citizenship, by way of emigration.

Today, I poise my *oud* on my thigh, I try to control the tremor in my fingers, and attempt to play my national anthem flawlessly, as I prepare for the trip to Canada. It's not a new beginning. There's no such thing. "There are just a series of endings," as the Egyptian novel *Hepta* says. The time has come for Yafa to write a happy ending to this journey of refuge. But first, to inhabit Yafa, I must swear an oath to an English queen in a cold land in the continent of North America.

I must become someone else to be myself.

Around twenty years ago, one of my brothers took the same path. At that time, Beirut's spaces had crowded him out and I asked him, at the age of six: "Why go?"

"Because we're refugees. They don't want us here and they don't like us."

"Why don't they like us? What did we do to them?"

"Not necessarily for any reason. They don't even like each other, so why should they like us?"

The story of a Palestinian is truly farcical. If you are Palestinian you can't live in Palestine, but if you take on a Western identity you can. However, the question remains, will you continue to be Palestinian? That's not what your papers say. That's my final source of melancholy: Could their foreign papers distract me from my goal?

What do I care about papers? Paper and ink are the greatest deceivers that a refugee might encounter. They're used to write international charters, and they pen our illegitimate refuge on paper that's as blue as the sea that was taken from us.

Fairuz can sing all she wants about "a small house in Canada." Today, I don't love Canada, and I don't hate Beirut. I know for certain that Beirut doesn't hate me, but I'm leaving regardless because I love Yafa. I was a dreamer when I was younger and I thought that I would one day walk barefoot to my country, from Ras al-Naqura in southern Lebanon to the shore of 'Akka in northern Palestine. But in reality the road can only pass through foreign countries, countries from which the children in their little hats flock to my country. They settle there and are annoyed by talk of Palestinian refugees in the camps of the diaspora.

The Forty-Day Cold Spell

"I think that today is my birthday."

"Happy birthday, Uncle!"

"Wait, did you say 'I think?'"

"Yes, indeed."

"Uncle, you don't know your own birthday?"

"Palestinians don't have specific birthdates, my dear. Haven't you ever examined your identity card or any of your personal documents?"

"Yes, I have, Uncle, and you're right, they just list the year of birth, no day, not even the month. I always wondered about that. So no one in the family remembers your birthdate?"

"Let me tell you. Like you, I remember the details of my childhood well, even things that happened before I was born. Your grandmother was pregnant with me when the attack began on the village of al-Kabri. But my mother, who was carrying me as well as the burden of their Nakba, was overloaded and couldn't walk any longer. She had to wait for her relatives to arrive in Lebanon and send back the donkey that had carried them there so that she could ride it to the village of Qana. When Palestinians arrived in

Lebanon, they set up tents and collapsed them repeatedly, moving from one area to another. They were so caught up in the whirlwind of days that they stopped measuring time; they had no calendars that could tell them the date, and the men were not free to register births and deaths. There were events more important than the children of the Nakba. So none of us knows when exactly we were born. All I know is that the weather was very stormy when I was born, with the strongest winds of any day that year. They were so strong that they pulled out the stakes holding down our tent. That's how the tent flew over my mother as she gave birth to me and the whole camp could watch her in labor. The women rushed in with sheets to cover up what the heavens wanted to expose. That's how I was born. I don't know when it was, but they call that part of the year 'the forty-day cold spell.' Of course, my dear, the iciness of the Nakba can't compare with the iciness of Canada."

About the Mug and the Planet

When my brother and I left Beirut in the direction of the frigid land, my mother cried all night. We were replaying the same scenario that our three brothers had acted out before us. We were the last children to leave her and she was struck with a painful case of déjà vu. Her only solace was that it would be the last farewell and that none further would be necessary.

My brother and I didn't carry much. We didn't want to be burdened with heavy memories. We decided, on separating from the stigma of refuge, that we would leave Beirut and its sorrows to its people.

That day, I wore a dark sweater that said "Palestine" in pretty ornate script in English and Arabic. Still, the Iraqi immigrants who were on the same flight insisted that we were Iraqi immigrants like them. I put that down to the similarity between the Palestinian refugee travel document and the passport provided by the United Nations to asylum seekers like them. I remember the little Iraqi Christian girl Anna, who had cancer and captivated us throughout the flight. I often wonder what happened to her: did the disease defeat her, or did she conquer it with that smile of hers? I dreaded the answer, and so I never found a way to contact her. I prefer to think that Anna was treated in Canada, recovered beautifully, and is playing hide-and-seek with little blond friends in the school playground.

In our stopover in the Cairo airport, I remember how you, my brother, accompanied me to every single shop in the duty-free zone in search of a mug to add to my collection. You were the only one who never made fun of my obsession with collecting trifles like mugs stamped with the names of countries, the Palestine supplement of *as-Safir* newspaper, commemorative buttons, and bottles filled with colored sand. We went to every store in that airport but we couldn't find a single mug with the word "Egypt." So before we left, we had to buy a cone-shaped mug with a pharaonic motif for eleven dollars! Later on, we bought a mug from the renowned Niagara Falls in Canada for a mere three dollars!

Do you remember those strange, isolated working-class cafés in the Cairo airport, with names like Lady's Café and Planet Café? We walked into the Planet Café and almost died from the fumes of cigarettes and water-pipes, and from the damp emanating from the old wooden chairs.

It was your first visit to Canada and, more importantly, the first time in fourteen years that you would see our brothers. Living half your life without seeing your brother is not easy. But the real difficulty was enduring the overwhelming emotions in the first moments of reunion. All the lounges of the Toronto airport were not spacious enough to hold our first four-way hug.

Everything about that trip was strange for us: from the calmness of the towns to the intensity of luxury. The cold winter spell that lasted forty days for us stretched nine months for them.

Exactly one year ago, to the day, I was the one who backtracked. Despite the identity cards that forgot our dates of birth, despite the blackness of my dark suit, despite the loss of Ramallah and my nonexistent wedding, I was the one who backtracked. I retraced my steps back to Beirut, alone, without you.

On my return trip to Beirut, I didn't stroll around the transit area, I didn't buy a mug, and I didn't drink anything at the Planet Café.

I haven't spoken to you since I came back. I haven't asked you how you're doing in that cold land. Why should I? I'm certain you're living a better life than the life of refuge.

But I miss you! We miss you: me, my mother, the mug, and the Planet!

Clutter

My mother, like every other Palestinian mother, measures her status in society by the level of tidiness of her household. Every time we brought what she classified as "unnecessary" new stuff into the house, she would make the same comment: "We don't need more clutter!" I don't know whether *barabish* ("clutter") is a Palestinian expression, or whether my mother invented it out of nowhere to express her dread of the copious quantities of books, newspapers, papers, photographs, and other stuff that we couldn't quite stash away tidily in compartments.

But my mom always had solutions. She would steal the newspapers and use them to wipe the glass or to line the trash bin. She'd say: "There are hundreds of newspapers, they'll never notice that one is missing." She'd tear up photographs. Digital photography is an undervalued blessing. You only appreciate it when, like me, you're unable to close your drawers because of the stacks of pictures, albums, and negative prints. Anyway, most of the pictures my mother tore up are ones of old friends whom she'd like to tear up in person. But, of course, she hangs on to pictures of her engagement and wedding, as well as those of herself and my father in the presence of the "the wise one" (George Habash), which are stored in a sacred album that no one dares touch.

Each time I came home, my mother would inspect the bags I was carrying and would lose her temper when she discovered all kinds of scraps I had collected from the city: a car license plate that I found in the trash, a board made of cork that I stealthily took from the bookstore window, or even a ticket discarded on the side of the road.

I still remember the day my father brought home an encyclopedia that he had seen advertised in a trade magazine. He was practically jumping for joy because it had been such a good deal. My mother blew up because she didn't need more books. She never knew what to do with the three bookshelves we had in different parts of the house. At one point, she stacked all the old, worn-out, and warped books in one bookshelf and put it on the eastern balcony, out of sight. As for the really damaged books, with torn covers and missing pages, she put them in a box and threw them out with the trash. Fortunately, my father saw the box outside the apartment door before the trash was collected and saved it from oblivion. After that, he didn't speak to my mother for five nights. But that didn't stop her from throwing out books and other things; she just did it without our knowing.

I was never strong enough to defy my mother's orders. I threw stacks of memories into the trash. I would not look too long at each paper before breaking my emotional tie to it. That's how I could coldly part with twenty-five years.

However, when Fadi crossed my path, he presented me with a solution to life's accumulations of clutter that defied every logical thing that I had ever considered. Fadi entered my head from a narrow door and proceeded to construct his cabinets inside it, a process that overturned all my thoughts—or perhaps just organized them.

Khazaaen ("cabinets") is the name of a project centered in Jerusalem that seeks to build a societal archive out of virtual cabinets that gather the ephemera of people's daily lives. These cabinets bear our names and contain our stories by holding copies of all the papers and documents—every advertisement, invitation, business card, or poster—that we've ever come across. Your cabinet is your own possession as well as being the property of everyone else, so that they can know your story and you can read theirs.

History will write of war and peace; it will describe the throwing of rice and the shooting of bullets. But it won't speak of Abdullah Lama, the doctor who attended to poor people in Burj al-Barajneh refugee camp and didn't collect a fee. It won't write about the students at Galilee School who printed manifestos outlining their demand to return to Palestine and distributed them in UNRWA schools, and who were then expelled. And it won't tell of how monsters began to infiltrate our refugee camps a long time ago without arousing anyone's attention.

Khazaaen is an effort to redirect that writer of history who omitted us, who never attended to us when we bade him to slow down. It will recount things to him that others won't.

Fadi's cabinets paved the road to return in my head. He said: "Even if the refugees don't return, their things will."

I wasn't able to return to Palestine, to Jaffa, but my stuff, my papers, and my stories are now in a cabinet bearing my name in Jerusalem.

One day, someone will wander around this digital archive in Jerusalem searching for truth in every corner, and as he opens a cabinet he'll say, "So that's how the Palestinians lived."

And one day I'll return to Jerusalem, open my cabinet, and read all of the stories it contains from the life that I lived in Lebanon. I'll tell my dearest one how I lived, far from her in exile. That's the sign that I once held in a protest march. Here's the one-thousand-lira ticket I used to ride the no. 12 bus each day to university. This is the invitation card for my graduation ceremony. And there's the poster that they hung in the camp the day that Abu 'Ammar (Yasir 'Arafat) died.

Nowadays I regret every piece of paper that I ever threw away voluntarily. What's wrong with clutter? Clutter turns out to have a home, *mama*.

Hanin (Longing)

HANIN MOHAMMAD RASHID

(b. Burj al-Shimali, Tyre, 1993)

You may encounter it in your heart, in spite of yourself, after it has made its way to your ears as you listen to a random song chosen by the taxi driver. It may take you unintentionally to a destination further than your own but closer to yourself. You might come across it at the beginning of a poem that someone wrote after parting without intending to revive old wounds, yours, his, or anyone else's who happens to read it. You might see it clearly, teetering on the face of a grieving mother whose face has been colored by the flag shrouding a tired body. It might have been a stupid bullet that pierced her pure heart before it could touch her son's chest and make him a martyr. That is longing (*hanin*), the word, the feeling, and the constant companion.

Obviously, we don't have the freedom to choose our own names, and nor do we generally possess the courage to change them later. We become attached to our name with its few letters, and it possesses us in turn. It imbues us with a great deal of self-assurance and self-indulgence. Our name precedes us everywhere and is the first thing we introduce ourselves with when meeting others. It's the first thing we write on the exam papers that can determine our futures. It's the word we love to hear most when uttered by our loved ones.

I've always been fascinated by the strange relationship that develops inadvertently between some of my acquaintances and their names. They transform a name into a path that must be taken no matter the cost. Amal (Hope), for example, goes to bed every night confident that reality will take her hopes more seriously with every passing day. While Amani (Dreams) carries in her flowery heart many of the desires that she yearns to fulfill and works diligently to achieve them. Whereas Halima (Patience) is always waiting tolerantly in expectation of a better future that would be deserving of her smile.

As for me, I admit with overwhelming joy and some satisfaction that my name has been my lot in life, bringing me love, power, and pain. This has pleased me since childhood, and it pleases me even more to think that my name now shares so much of what I've lived through and what has lived in me. I'll try to write some of this down, if words don't fail me.

Each one of us has—whether we like it or not—a special longing (*hanin*) that occupies one or two sections of our heart. This longing sometimes pierces the isolation of night without prior invitation, leaping like a gazelle into a distracted consciousness, making matters worse and evoking painful memories. It's a longing that comes over and transforms you into a dumb icon. Because of it, you might weaken considerably in a place where only the strong exist, or you might forgive excessively in a place where you won't find someone who would ignore your most minor lapse.

Nevertheless, I laugh spontaneously whenever I relate the reason for my name. My sister, who is six years and one month older than me, was a huge fan of a certain cartoon character when she was a little girl. So she decided when I was born at the end of a gentle September to give me the name of the girlfriend of her cartoon hero. Thank God she didn't go overboard and call me "Rami," which was the name of the superhero himself!

That's how longing came to live with me, due to no fault of my own, thanks to my sister. I was fated to have that name ever since the first encounter between a man and woman who knew love at an early age and chose to be united by it. It was such a great passion that my mother is incapable of uttering a word about it whenever we ask her for details. She just makes do with a shy smile that I'll never understand. Longing adhered to me even though my mother had five children who preceded me into life, each of whom has left me with a small memory, which I searched for and collected during the period of nearly nine months I spent in my mother's kind and caring womb. I later wished that that womb had held me and carried me longer, as long as possible.

I was barely alive when my ears first picked up the scattered notes of a voice that was suitable for anything but singing. That voice was my father's, and he never tired of making us listen to a song whose lyrics never fail to instill in any solid citizen a mixture of pride, enthusiasm, and surprise. It was a song that my father had learned by heart, by mind, and by soul. And we learned it too, my siblings and I, without making any effort or exerting ourselves in any way.

There was no greater mystery for me than this song and others like it when I was young, and I tried my utmost later on to discover the secret behind it. It took some time and knowledge, and many late nights imbued with intimate memories, when my father transported us back to a time of contentment, determination, and sacrifice. In that time, my father's most fervent aim was to come home bringing a good omen for his mother, who had pinned all her hopes on her second son. She was the one who gave him the responsibility of achieving that aim.

So it was that I took my first steps in a special world of longing, a permanent longing for the homeland. The notes of my father's favorite song used to echo through our small house, and from there to the modest neighborhood in the small camp, and from there to the villages of southern Lebanon that we visited each month, the front and back seats of the car vibrating to the sounds of countless vocal concerts. There we would find fields of green spread out to meet the blueness of the sky, creating a beautiful, hope-inspiring tableau.

In a single, unwavering voice, we would sing: "I will confront you, my enemy, from every house, neighborhood, and street." We would let our voices loose and my father would unleash a stream of memories that refused to die or be reborn.

I don't remember ever asking about the meaning of those words. Sometimes a little girl might not do the expected thing. She may refrain from bothering anyone with her curiosity and inquisitiveness—who was she to ask what her father wanted to "confront"? Maybe the longing that my father harbored in his heart for the days when he was known as a *fida'i* didn't hide for very long and made its appearance in broad daylight. Our destination on those regular trips was not arbitrary but responded to that longing, reanimating the memory of the years he had spent in those parts.

My father seemed to live in the recesses of his memory more than he did in the present, and his dream to fulfill his mother's dream, which was the whole universe in his eyes, still overtook him from time to time.

My father took nothing from the rugged mountains where he encamped for many long, hard years, except a certain hardness. He took nothing from the nights he kept a lone vigil and uttered a prayer that could have been his last, except a terrible stillness. When that stillness settled over the features of his tan face, which betrayed his age, my siblings and I knew at once that something had certainly happened.

He was the righteous son, the second son of a modest family that had settled in their beloved Burj al-Shimali refugee camp, a refuge that they assumed to be temporary, and we inherited that assumption from them.

He was not lucky enough to have the name of his village recorded as his birthplace on his blue identity card, the most prized possession of every refugee, a label whose honor and anguish are acquired without any personal effort.

Everyone who knows my father knows that his journey of struggle and his repeated long absences in 1969 would not have been possible were it not for certain dawn prayers that protected him, a pure heart that gave him abundant love and attention, and an astute mind that realized the grave dangers that surrounded him. His mother chose to give to Palestine a piece of her heart and body in the hope that the occupation would be deterred by a revolution of young people protected by the eye of God and the hearts of their mothers.

My father's pulse never lost the rhythm given by those he loved and was loved by, and by the warm home within whose walls he spent so many evenings and transitioned from a troubled childhood to a hardly less troubled adolescence.

But his greatest longing was always reserved for the only woman who was irreplaceable for him: my grandmother, may she rest in peace.

It was a sacred relationship to a woman, whose features some say I share, with her pale cheeks and warm smile.

She wasn't a woman who rocked the cradle, as the saying goes, for the simple reason that she never owned one, but she shook the earth with her strength and insight, and she shook hearts with her gentle speech and the generosity she showed to strangers.

Her prayers she transformed into a steady bridge that my father could cross to fulfill her dream of victory and liberation of the homeland. She was unwavering in her support and encouragement, patting the shoulders that carried burdens and responsibilities exceeding the capacity of a lifetime, until she left us for good without anyone having informed her of the date of victory and return. She, in turn, told no one how painful it had been for her and her heart, which was small in size and large in love, to endure the lack of return.

I can recall all of the times my father paused during our evening talks to wipe away a stinging tear and to dampen the fervor of a longing evoked unintentionally by memories when we asked him about my grandmother.

My father once told us—after a moment's silence to catch his breath—that one night in 1976 he had gone back to his house in the camp to say what might be a last farewell and to commit to memory the faces of his loved ones. He and his comrades had been recruited for an important military mission on the hills overlooking Palestine. He remembered well how he hugged my grandmother and kissed her hand, while trying to hide the tears that were flowing spontaneously. My grandmother was in turn trying to give my father some comfort and hope with faint smiles, while her heart writhed in pain, all the while assuring him that the liberation of the land could only come about by the efforts of the young people from the camp. She followed him outside, wiping his brow with her palm and repeating a prayer: "May God bring you victory, my son."

I don't know why it was so hard for my father to relate such details from his love story with his homeland, which he lived with his whole body. His heart just broke when he did.

Maybe the pain of memories was so great that it imposed silence. There's no power greater than the power of memory; it has a way of awakening dormant pains down to the very last. There's no blaming the silent killer who doesn't take your leave when he kills but who accompanies you wherever you may be, whom you bear like a tattoo on your skin. It's a longing that never shrinks but deepens, despite our best efforts.

My father continues his story, ignoring for once the tears from his honey-colored eyes. I envy him when he speaks proudly about the numerous victories he registered in his youth, which turned him into a tireless and loyal lover of the homeland and the cause until his last breath. It carved into his memory many scenes that he struggled to put behind him when they were over, scenes that we found hard to imagine.

How can my imagination, which I've worked diligently to nurture and enrich, conjure up the image of my grandmother, whom I never really knew, as she gave him her blessing before he left to report to a military camp in the south?

He describes her voice, which he misses sorely, as one that skillfully hid her sadness and apprehension.

My grandmother said: "Son, please tell them not to hang your picture in front of our house if you die a martyr. I don't want to see your picture torn on the walls, I want it to remain pristine in my eyes and my heart."

How can I explain what lies behind such fortitude and power, which just grew with every goodbye? How did my grandmother summon all that affection mixed with strength to transform my father, the indefatigable *fida'i*, into a glorious man who only weakened before her and never broke except when she was mentioned? Nothing could stop his heart except my grandmother's departure thirty years ago.

My grandmother's longing for her birthplace grew to the point that she was unable to hide it any longer and she became incapable of living out the rest of her days. Longing took her from us and harshly wrested her hand away from my father's, leaving his fingers holding emptiness. They were both victims of loneliness seeking something to fill the spaces between them.

My grandmother departed, leaving all those who knew her searching for someone to console them as her last kisses, her warmth still enveloped them from every direction.

Halima, may she rest in peace, was my grandfather's first love, my father's deepest love, and the love in whose memory I was raised. I never had a share of it in her presence, but I learned all those years to gaze at her hanging picture and to pronounce the word "*Sitti*" without hesitation or pain.

Death refuses to be gentle and leaves us crying for our weak selves, not for those who've left us, training ourselves to cope with inescapable loss and the sudden memories that longing awakens.

Death, whose destructive and unexpected impact I was never aware of until I experienced it a little over a year ago. I awoke from a beloved sleep to a yet more beloved voice, except that voice was weeping and wailing. My mother had just heard the news of her elder sister's death and had begun to mourn in the way that befits a great love and a deep relationship.

My darling aunt had received more than her share of my strange longing, attachment, and sympathy. There are two scenes that come most readily to mind featuring my aunt and myself as the heroines, in which everyone else was just an extra and everything around us just pretty scenery. The first scene occurred in April 1996, when I was just three years old and the spoiled baby of the household, playing and enjoying the company of my elder siblings, in typical fashion, who loved me as I loved them. My aunt and her family, which was a large one, sought refuge in our house in the camp when they fled from the Israeli assault on southern Lebanon known as the "Grapes of Wrath." But the real grapes of wrath burst inside me, for reasons I still can't explain. I was overcome with feelings of jealousy and confinement. A child like me couldn't accept the presence of long-term guests in a small house that was her only arena for playing, frolicking, dancing, and chasing the ants in the corners.

My senseless antics made me laugh when they were related to me later by my siblings and mother. I was humiliated when they told me about my chronic stomachache and unexplained constipation. It was as though I had pledged to my intestines not to enter a toilet for as long as my aunt and her children were in our house. This was confirmed when I ran like lightning to the bathroom at the very moment that our dear guests left.

Even though the second scene contradicts the first, it was also one in which my aunt, me, and war were the principal characters. It was July 2006 and, once again, my aunt and her family sheltered in our house from the shelling that was following them everywhere, even in the refugee camp. But this time, whenever I heard sounds of bombardment, whether near or far, I would search frantically for my aunt whose presence I had rejected so strenuously when I was younger. I sought her out all over the house, held tightly to her arm, and buried my terrified face in her lap while she writhed—not due to fear but to the discomfort I gave her by clinging so tightly to her. With every tug of her arm, she would try to calm me down, all the while whispering: "Hanin, my dear, my shoulder. My shoulder, my dear."

I have no idea how my initial rebuff turned into affection over the years, or how her face and slightly hoarse voice turned into fragments of memory that will haunt my heart forever. My search for a shoulder to lean on will likely continue throughout my life, with death being the surest reminder that the shoulders and hands we manage to find are bound to disappear.

Talk of longing can seem so tedious when it is joined with absence and parting. But it can be just the opposite, spreading hope and light laughter, when it is connected with your first steps toward a world of deep sentiment, a world in which there is no will except the will of love.

Praise the Lord! A heart the size of your fist, composed of flesh and blood, can hold enough passion to supply the entire planet if it happens to be inhabited by longing. Even if you're strong enough to withstand emotion you will likely not be able to resist attaching yourself intensely to everything related to whoever is responsible for that upheaval of the heart. You automatically lose the ability to control the present that is lived for the sake of one person and the future that doesn't seem beautiful or even desirable except in that person's presence.

Out of nowhere, a soul that you meet and befriend transports you from one place to another without your moving at all. It embraces you in a way that a thousand hugs are unable to do and renders the rest of the world entirely superfluous. It alone is capable of cracking the code of your special universe, and it is uniquely able to occupy everything within you at every time and in every place. When the owner of that soul becomes a cherished guest, they add longing to longing and ignite your spirit with fondness.

I'm a little ashamed to admit the sense of strangeness and warmth that settled over me when I discovered that with each encounter, I took a step forward in life, and with each parting, I took two steps backward. I felt it when I saw that same face in the faces of passersby in the early morning, or when I heard that same voice in a song I chanced to listen to at night.

That feeling is the harbinger of a looming storm of longing. I never cared about the aftermath that I would ordinarily have dreaded. But my constant certainty that it would eventually pass, fade away, and that the clamor would subside, was what softened the ordeal. It also allowed whoever had ignited the flame inside me to cross effortlessly toward me as though there were no obstacles in the way.

At one time, I felt as though it was too late for me to experience and live all this passionate chaos; beautiful things had lost their way and would never approach me. But then they collided with me all at once without causing any pain.

After longing took up residence in Hanin, a thousand sentiments in one heart, at long last someone arrived to spread calm and serenity. My affections developed in much the same way as any creature in this world, without any effort on my part.

They developed in the pupils of the eyes, under the eyelids, and among the lashes, each one of which I memorized. In the grip of fingers that I always loved to embrace, and in the polish of nails whose colors he admired. In the heart of a small child we dreamed of bringing together into the world, who would grow up with us, among the pages of a book we both read and loved. On a pillow that I replaced every now and then.

My affections grew and my longing increased, beyond what my friends had expected or my mother had hoped, even beyond my own rosiest dreams.

A crazy longing accompanies me now, too, and it has done so for days, as I collect missing pieces of myself that have been scattered for too long. I gather them up and string them into a beautiful necklace around my neck, to remind me of the faithfulness of our two hearts, a string of jasmine flowers that persists despite the vagaries of the seasons.

I'm sustained by my great faith in the mercy of God that encompasses our weak hearts and by a saying that I repeat whenever I need some special solace: "Everything happens for a reason, and there is no room for coincidence in our destiny." I'm now capable of accepting any ending and living with fragments of memories. I can tolerate the bitter taste of loneliness along with a sip of the coffee that I've lately become addicted to.

Longing always presides over everything else. It visits me suddenly when I innocently shut my eyes like a child and let my frail memory take me back to a recurring scene. I used to take a narrow road from our neighborhood to the girls' school in the camp. This road witnessed many scenes in the life of Hanin the child, the adolescent, and even the adult. My sisters and friends and I would pause in the middle of an alleyway when we overheard a conversation among members of a family in one of the narrow houses whose walls were indistinguishable from those of the house next door. This eavesdropping—a nasty habit—was one of our many special morning rituals. Mornings in the camp were disturbed only by the smells of food being prepared early, or the cries of a newborn baby. Puddles of water adorned our path in all seasons, not just winter, and we were accustomed to hopping over them gracefully despite the weight of our backpacks to avoid getting soaked and humiliated.

We never felt the distance, blissfully unaware of our slow pace until the school bell rang out announcing the imminent locking of the big blue metal door. At that point, we'd start running as though a starting gun had sounded for a race. We fell in line hurriedly as we expelled the cold air from our lungs, along with the words that had gone unspoken and the laughter that had to be suppressed until the end of the school day. Like bees in a hive or soldiers on parade, we'd begin to sing the national anthem in loud, strong voices. As our teacher used to say: "I want the sound to shake the earth."

At that point, our school could have been the hallowed ground of a battlefield and we, a bunch of sleepy schoolgirls, might have been a group of resurgent *fida'i*s.

Years passed as I replayed the same scene in my head. That is where I was born and that is how I grew up, and everything grew up with me, just so.

In the beginning, longing for me was restricted to the members of my family, a family that I enjoyed being the youngest member of. Then longing extended to a homeland to which I dreamt of returning, and from there to dear ones who had been taken by death, leaving only a picture or two to kiss whenever I missed them. Then longing extended to a small refugee camp inhabited by simple people, a place that was the origin of all beginnings and that made me what I am now. And then longing developed and I became enmeshed in it, when my heart was touched by a soul mate and a partner in dream and reality. At that point, longing outgrew all description, and love outpaced all happiness. I came to love life through him and myself and planted flowers in his image wherever I went.

I imagine longing lurking in the shadows, contemplating the finishing touches on a story of the reawakening of an old wound. One of many stories that takes so much time and so many sleepless nights to create. Longing is always revealing its skill at locating the sites of wounds that don't heal and choosing the most difficult times to accept loss. Longing scatters some salt on the wound and proceeds on its way, leaving behind the traces of love, or something similar, which remain with us for life. We ache while longing laughs at the end of every night, relishing the victory and revealing a smiling countenance.

Didn't I say at the beginning that longing resides in your heart in spite of yourself?

It lives in the love of each of us for ourselves, in the details of life that leave deep traces upon us. It lives in our love of the past and of those who dwelt in the past, in those who left us without saying goodbye and took parts of us with them. It lives in the love of a mother for her son, in her fear for him and her anticipation of his return. It lives in a son's undying love for a mother who is long gone and whose shining face accompanies him wherever he goes. It lives in the homeland you grew up in even though you never set foot there, and in the love for a road in the camp that is only wide enough for two friends. It lives in the love that you make sure to express to whoever inhabits your heart.

Longing alone always increases and never diminishes, it can persist and endure after everything else has ended.

My Heart Hangs from a Mulberry Tree

WEDAD TAHA

(b. Libya, 1991)

Large raindrops are reflected on the dashboard of the car and I mistake them for insects that must have crept in when I wasn't looking. I try to wipe the shiny black dots with my hand, shivering in the December chill, and succeed in wiping nothingness. I shake my head, ashamed at myself, at the delusions that overcome me. I'm cowardly to the point of being mortally afraid of an insect, and always so alienated from my surroundings. Let me be clear: I've always been at arm's length from everything around me and also from myself. I don't really know myself, maybe because I haven't searched for myself. But nor have I attached myself to a place or a person; I've never been enthusiastic about anything or been driven to seek reasons. I just walk with my head to the ground.

I never knew that Palestine was my homeland until I came to Lebanon. Maybe I realized that I was Palestinian late in life, or maybe I didn't fully appreciate what it meant to be Palestinian until I wandered. From where they lived in south Lebanon, my family went in search of life in the farthest reaches of the earth. After my parents got married, they went to Libya, where I was born. From there, we went to the United Arab Emirates, where we lived until I was twelve. I don't remember my parents mentioning Palestine once. Instead, in our house, all the talk was about the refugee camp. I didn't understand the word and I wasn't interested enough to ask. I was too caught up in my childhood: school field trips, my green velvet dress, my lost canteen, and the gold ring that I took from my mother's jewelry box to give to my teacher, which she returned when she saw my father's initials written on it in tiny turquoise stones. I don't recall my father ever sticking to one job, so we lived a simple, basic life in the UAE. When he worked, we would eat and live comfortably, and when he lost his job, my mother would shed tears and sell some of her gold jewelry. We didn't come back to Lebanon every summer, as immigrants do nowadays. I don't know if my parents wanted to distance themselves, or if their limited means prevented them from going. All I know is that I was a stubborn child who loved dancing and my Sudanese friend Mahira, who was separated from me forever and without a goodbye when we left.

I'm not sure if the first Gulf War was the reason my father lost his job. Abu 'Ammar (Yasir 'Arafat) exposed thousands of Palestinians to expulsion and displacement from countries that sought to punish him for his position in favor of Saddam Hussein. Thousands were deported and driven out callously at that time, and that's when we returned to Lebanon.

I understood the meaning of displacement, loss, and longing for the first time when my mother said goodbye to me at the door of my grandfather's house in the al-Raml neighborhood in the southern Lebanese city of Tyre. My heart ached that day. I didn't realize that she would only be returning at distant and intermittent intervals. I didn't know whether the need for me not to miss out on school was the only reason I had to be separated from her and from my siblings for a whole year, or whether it was my uncle Mahmud's death of a sudden heart attack in Germany at the age of twenty-eight that broke her to the point that she forgot me there.

My mother is a woman constructed out of fear. It's a fear that I came to resent as I grew older. I never understood the reason for it, and she wasn't self-aware enough to explain her phobias to me. All she knew was that the traditions she inherited dictated that I obey her and that her being my mother gave her the right to fence me in with her thoughts. I never forgave her for that. I never accepted the inane habits whose only goal, as far as I could tell, was to make me stupid. But my rebellion was purely passive. I sought refuge in my heart, though I don't know whether this rescued me from my mother's traditions and her distant refugee camp, or whether it somehow succeeded in entrenching them in me more deeply.

In Lebanon, I went to school with my cousins, with whom I shared a room in my grandfather's house, even though my two aunts considered me to be their guest and set aside space for me in their cold bedroom. Their room overlooked the Yunis hair salon and I would look out furtively from their small, secret window to satisfy my curiosity about what went on there, amidst all the mirrors that covered the walls. I've always been drawn to tight mysterious spaces and fascinated by every crevice in every place I've visited, always searching for signs of life in them. I was attracted to passageways like the narrow alley that we took daily to and from the Nimrin school in al-Buss refugee camp. As I stumbled through that mud-covered alleyway all winter long, I would be overcome with many fears. I yearned for school yet was anxious that I might encounter a cat that would brush up against my leg.

Along the way to school, we passed buildings, other schools, small rosebushes, and reddish, rusty iron gates leading to dark houses, which opened in the mornings to let women out into the alleyway. The women would greet one another, say goodbye to their children, and sweep the rainwater away from their low thresholds toward the gutter that flowed very close by. Open gutters were everywhere in the camp, and we would skip over them as they emanated fetid smells of coffee grounds and the mulberry leaves that fell from the giant trees nearby. They called it the mulberry camp.

On the way to school, I would meet up with my relative Ikram, with her fair hair, turquoise-colored eyes, and raspy voice. We'd recite yesterday's lesson together as we admired the spring flowers or braved the December wind, pushing past throngs of schoolkids who crowded the alleyways of al-Buss camp. I never knew how she managed to find shortcuts that brought us to school earlier than anyone else. That gave me a chance to observe the school silently before it echoed to the sounds of shouting children and the ringing of the golden bell wielded by the principal. I've retained the habit as an adult, arriving to work an hour before the start of the school day. I read, drink coffee, and take in the morning and my dreams.

The black school gate was huge. We entered through a narrow side door, and I would lower my head to clear it as the principal looked on with a paternal smile. His hair was always carefully combed to the side, the part placed a good deal too close to his ear. That's all I remember about him, apart from his short leather jacket. A picture comes to mind now from the recesses of my memory: the principal is presenting me with a prize for academic excellence, with his usual smile, as everyone looks on with evident satisfaction. I don't remember the experience itself or my feelings in the moment, but I will never forget my grandfather's face at home. His white beard was glistening and his pink gums peeked out from under his bushy mustache. He teased me, as I squirmed, gullible and clueless. He tapped his cane with glee, saying: "What have you done at school today, darling?" He asked that alarming question and allowed the silence to linger between us, just to torment me. Then he said: "I saw Mr. Muhammad today. Why didn't you tell me you came first in school?" A few moments passed. I still didn't understand that he was trying to make me happy and revel in my success. The full significance of my achievement didn't sink in until I got beaten up by my younger cousin, who was my grandfather's favorite and who was driven crazy by all the attention and indulgence that I was receiving from him.

My grandfather then called the whole family over: "Yusra, come, my dear! Maha! Taha! Where are you, kids? Mustafa's daughter has made me proud today! Come get some *bonbon*!" He rolled the last word on his tongue in a way that prompted us to laugh and imitate him behind his back. Then he grabbed his precious bag of goodies and poured the contents over our heads. The colored candy nuggets flew everywhere as I reached upward to grab as much as I could.

I don't know where I acquired a curiosity about place names. When I learned that my school was named after a village in Palestine, I pestered my grandfather with questions about Nimrin. But I never thought to ask him about the blue flag hanging from the pole outside, or about the blue windows, cold seats, and dark rooms of our school, which was considered a model compared to other UNRWA schools. My love of reading first surfaced in the UAE. My mother would buy us copies of a children's magazine, *Majid*, which I read with excitement, rereading them over and over, without ever tiring of the repetition. In Tyre, I started reading my schoolbooks for pleasure. I especially loved history, and craved the praise of my history teacher, who used to say "Bravo" every time I showed signs of prowess. I once asked my grandfather what the word meant and he chuckled loudly, his full, firm belly shaking until the white *hattah* fell from his head and he had to pick it up and rearrange it with the black *'iqal*. I followed the movement of his hands, waiting for him to explain the meaning of the word, but he never responded.

My question remained hanging when my beloved teacher Kamil passed on a few years later. I couldn't comprehend how someone so tall could die. His mysterious and frightening death, along with that of my uncle, may have prompted my first questions about death. I realized that death could be trivial sometimes, yet permanent. God is ingenious at creating pretexts to draw us closer to him. He can make death sudden in a scary, perplexing, and devastating way. That's how I felt, anyway, when my mother said goodbye to another brother, who was handsome, kind, and full of life. He visited us one last time in a coffin carried all the way from his cold exile.

"Mama, I want to be veiled," I said to my mother absentmindedly when she came to visit me, as I buried my little head in her lap. I shut my eyes and took in the scent from her long black dress. It was my mother's scent and lap. She hadn't visited me in a month and a half, leaving me to toss and turn at night, yearning and longing for her. I missed her dear spirit and missed playing with my siblings. I was the middle child, but I always behaved like a mother to them. I cried for an hour as I buried myself in her lap and held on to her, as though I was trying to plant her in my soul so that I could have my fill of her. My mother was and has always been my comfort and the soul of my soul. I'm not sure whether being deprived of her made me more attached to her, or whether it was her short stories, or her sweet singing that mingled with the steam and smell of soap when she bathed us. I held her head with my hand and told her not to leave me there, to take me with her, wherever that might be. I couldn't stop crying. I didn't know where I stood or how to make sense of what was happening to me. I wasn't fully conscious of the significance of what I had lived through.

One of the clearest images that I had came from my dreams. Like most Palestinian families, mine was pious, following traditions inspired by the face of God and his power over hearts, minds, and practices. Did I just say the "face" of God? It was a face that I saw through thick, high, white clouds, an ethereal face that visited me in a dream and I spoke to it. I don't remember what He said, but He spoke to me too. Yes, I spoke to God when I was asleep, and in the same dream I saw the prophet. When I woke up in a muddled state and said, "Mama, I want to be veiled," my mother refused. She feared that I would take off the veil after a while, and she wanted me to be sure of the first free decision that I would make. Did I say "free decision"? I don't know how free my decision was, nor do I know the meaning of that idea now. I don't even know if it was a decision, or just the outcome of the traditions speaking to me in a dream.

All the women around me were veiled. My grandmother was veiled, despite the fact that she continued to flirt with my grandfather into her seventies. My mother was veiled, covering the most beautiful hair of any woman—apart, perhaps, from the hair of nymphs, if they exist—with its waves and thick locks that fell in layers, and its magical, saturated color. I always contrasted it with the thin and wiry hair of my paternal aunts, and I thanked God that I didn't inherit theirs. All four of my aunts, and all the women of the neighborhood, were veiled. Even Umm Sulayman in her dark, cramped hole in the wall wore a headscarf, though she never went out and was hardly capable of walking. She had barely any visitors except me, my grandmother, her daily plate of food, the ravages of winter, her grinding poverty, and the memories of her children.

For my first veiled photograph, I smiled before the lens of Ibrahim al-Susi, posing in front of a white background. I sent the picture to my father along with a keychain engraved with the words: "If hearts could be gifted, I would have given you mine." I didn't expect much of a reply, but one sunny winter's day the school principal summoned me. As soon as I crossed the threshold of his office, I saw my father perched giantlike on the black leather couch. I threw myself at him and was pricked by his thick black mustache. He and the principal chuckled at how long I cried, then he kissed me. I felt special because my father had come to pick me up before the end of the school day. It was a rare and strange event. When we got home, my grandfather was resplendent in his usual chair in the living room. There was a lunch in honor of my father, who then took me to our new house. We arrived there exhausted after a long car ride on a road full of potholes, my insides rattled by all the vibrations. The road had gone on and on, scenes of fruit orchards rushing past fleetingly, as my heart raced gleefully, soaking up the exhilaration of the day. As soon as the car stopped, I ran toward the house and took in the aroma of the lentil dish that my mother was preparing especially for me.

In between two refugee camps, and in the face of an impossible return, my grandfather had bought a small plot of land with the money transfers that my father had sent back while he was working in the Gulf. On it, he'd built a two-story house, which he only managed to enjoy in his final years. The bloody events that had consumed Lebanon, including the Palestinians, rendered the house hostage to a variety of factions, militias, and groups. Some of them turned it into a sniper's nest because of its location on a main artery between the camps of 'Ayn al-Hilweh and al-Miyeh wa Miyeh, and it also served as a Lebanese army barracks and a main hospital of the Palestinian Red Crescent. Others turned it into an ammunition depot. Our neighbors even told us that during some periods of the war it had become a makeshift prison.

My mother was the first to see our new home in that building. She says she almost fainted when she went inside. I can only imagine her crushing disappointment and sense of loss as she saw her years of life in the Gulf devastated by the greed of the militias and others who had plundered our property. My grandfather had registered the house in his name and it was to be inherited by my father and paternal uncles after his death. The bizarre thing is that the house is still being held hostage. During Rafiq Hariri's term as prime minister, the Lebanese parliament passed a property law prohibiting Palestinians from owning land in Lebanon, so when my grandfather died, none of his children were able to inherit the property or register the house in their names. That building, where we spent over twenty years, until I convinced my father of the need for change, now seems cursed to me.

After completing intermediate school, I enrolled in the girls' public high school in Saida, now called Yumna al-'Id School. I joined a group of unusually intelligent and determined students. I never understood why, in my second year of high school, I was made to share the prize for academic excellence with a Lebanese schoolmate of mine, when I felt that I was the one who'd earned it. When I received the award, the principal insisted that the modest prize money be split between me and my schoolmate Hiba. My mother was nevertheless delighted with my success and used the small sum to enroll my sister at the UNRWA Beisan School, which had suddenly started charging fees. It wasn't the first time that I felt that God somehow wanted us to be educated despite our dire circumstances. Many Palestinians took scholarships from the political factions, but we never sought their help. I'm not sure if this was because of my parents' sense of pride, or simply their determination to keep us as far from that scene as possible.

I often felt that my sense of identity had been suspended. I never grasped the value of attending a meeting of the Palestinian students' association at university, or becoming a member of an organization, or marching in a protest, or pledging allegiance to a leader. Perhaps it's just that my sense of belonging to Palestine was a private thing. My love of my homeland was a little like my prayers to God, which I would even hide from my own self if I could. But I've always had a sense of unexplainable alienation and unsettling isolation. This has followed me my whole life and been compounded with each trial I've experienced.

It was no different when I went to work for an UNRWA school after I graduated from university. For some reason, I always had an overwhelming conviction that I would never work in an UNRWA school. The very existence of the agency felt like a source of shame to me. I refused to benefit from any of its services. It might have been my sense of superiority or my patriotism. Or it might have been my denial of reality, the facts of Palestinian futility, destitution, and dispersal, and the utter dependence on a job, a bag of flour, or a blanket that revealed our nakedness and the ills of the world. But this very same rejection of neediness is what led me to accept a job as a substitute teacher at an agency that views us through the prism of deprivation. Perhaps I didn't have a better alternative at the time, or perhaps I couldn't bear to disappoint my parents anymore. The job seemed to offer material and moral compensation for the many small tragedies that defined their lives and our lives together.

Our house and my identity weren't the only things that were suspended and liminal in my life; my experience of war was also virtual. I never lived war in the true sense. My mother never led us down to the bomb shelters, as did many other Palestinian women with their families. No one ever died right next to me and I was never forced to walk over dead bodies, as had the people of Tal al-Za'tar refugee camp. But war dwelled in me through the stories of my mother, who was traumatized by its horrors. My mother never ceased to mention war and she had no shortage of stories about it. My only close contact with war was during Operation Grapes of Wrath, the Israeli war on Lebanon in 1996, when our house filled up with refugees fleeing from Tyre to Sidon to escape the Israeli assaults. We all piled into the large bedroom that was my parents'. We children giggled and squabbled, as children do. And the adults feared hunger, as adults do. Once I heard the adults haggle with the young men distributing rations. They claimed that their numbers warranted more loaves of bread, while the men said that they were just trying to exploit the war like everyone else, pleading refugee status to claim more than their fair share. That's when I heard my uncle's widow cry out with evident frustration: "Have you ever seen me here before?"

Longing is the song of the downtrodden. My grand-mother used to sing; she sang to everything: to the pillow and the sea, to long roads and forgotten threshing floors, to henna and weddings. But I was never aware that she sang to Palestine. I never asked her. I'd hear her humming and listen closely, and when she choked on her own longing, she would trail off and I would stop. Perhaps her fluent singing and her silent tears taught me restraint. Perhaps her gentle voice introduced me to my homeland. Perhaps she gave me a conflicted image of Palestinians: meek and mild, but cursed. It's true, I blamed Palestinians for their complicity with the occupation. If only they hadn't left Palestine for the Israelis to take. If they hadn't surrendered and weakened, we wouldn't have been displaced. We paid a heavy price for displacement—our dignity degraded by time and compromises. We've made desperate attempts to assert our existence without realizing the magnitude of the concessions, betrayal,

and treachery that constantly and repeatedly expose us, generation after generation, to humiliation.

These feelings became further entrenched when I
worked for UNRWA. A Palestinian in Lebanon is not considered a human being worthy of life, which has led Palestinians
to revere UNRWA as worshippers believe in prayers, simply
because it provides them with some basic services. It was
there that I first got the idea in my head that Palestinians
are their own worst enemies, that they're masochists, full of
pathologies, that they suffer from mental disorders, including a kind of emotional stinginess. I put this down to the
horrors that afflicted our collective consciousness and spread
to our culture. Stinginess is a result of deprivation and fear
of want, and a miser is first and foremost stingy with their
feelings and emotions.

In the teachers' lounges at UNRWA schools, all you
hear about are salaries and compensation. In the classrooms,
all you see are curses and punishment. If you don't use cor-
poral punishment you're considered stupid. That's where I
first felt a rift developing between myself and my Palestinian
surroundings. They had grim faces, the UNRWA teachers,
and some of them had been my teachers in middle school.
But the schools are also where I got to know the hearts of the
children and took a measure of their suffering. Despite my
rage at daily life in the schools, they also taught me empathy
and appreciation for everything I raged against and all that
pained me in Palestinian society. For a million reasons, my
society was fragmented and incoherent, not least because it
lacked a clear and tangible image of the homeland and a solid
sense of citizenship. Our image of Palestine is vague to the
point of vanishing. Our sense of belonging is toxic to the

point of deadly conflict, exclusion, and rejection. Factions loom large and leaders are mythologized, while the homeland recedes behind disguises and our trivial daily realities.

I mentioned the hearts of the children. Their little hands shoot upward with excitement, as though toward God, as they shout out to you: "Me, Miss . . . me, me, me . . ." I would look at them and resent the teachers who could bring themselves to strike those delicate little petals. That would prompt me to ask myself a series of Sisyphean questions like Who am I? Who are we? and What is our destiny? that would send my head spinning. I didn't know who I was, who God was, or even what it meant to be Palestinian—except that it meant tasting bitterness and being marginalized. It meant being ashamed of being human, being weak and expelled from your homeland. It meant accepting the achievements of leaders who only existed to commit idiocies, who confirmed your loss and squandered your rights. It meant feeling an uncomfortable satisfaction about burdening others with your tragedy and making them pay the price of your exile. To them, you're a blight on the conscience of the world, a world that witnessed your tragedy and remained silent.

I really felt that Palestinians *had* burdened the world with their plight, a plight that they sometimes participated in creating and other times did not. When I saw myself surrounded by colleagues whose only concerns were money and political factions, and when I found that Palestine as a nation was completely absent from their discussions, it made me think that our intifada (uprising) should really be against ourselves. Our attempts to blackmail a world that consecrated our loss with indifference and complicity made us more like the Israelis, who glorify themselves. Despite our victimhood, we haven't asked the world for material compensation for our dispersal or for the quotidian massacres that have been committed against us for more than half a century. Still, our attempts at blackmail only succeed in making the homeland more distant. They consecrate our humanitarian reality to the point that we forget ourselves and the nation, and we're left with no vision of what is to come.

I won't deny that I was overly idealistic. I was harsh on myself and my people, demanding of us a high level of awareness and neglecting to realize that we're all only human. I demanded change while everyday reality was sealing our fate. Maybe I failed at times to see that we had a right to live far from lofty goals. Maybe I failed to see that those whom I criticized were fighting their own small battles in life. They were just employees given instruction by more senior employees in the name of serving the community of nations. Maybe I failed to ask myself whether it was possible for us Palestinians, after all the Arab and international treachery and the internal betrayal, to live free. Whether it was possible for us to overcome our fear, ignorance, and disorientation. Whether we didn't have to wait for some twist of fate to give us the right to lead normal lives, preoccupied only with complaints about roads and infrastructure, or bureaucracy and red tape, or better telephone service, water, and electricity. I don't know whether it's possible, after sixty-nine years of dispersal, to choose anything but whatever is available or possible. I don't know whether we're able to climb down from our cross of suffering to become a people. But some sincere efforts here and there, by a driver who was once a prisoner, or a child learning, or a wedding or birth, made me realize that our resistance to Israel and our struggle for existence begin and end in our hearts. This line of thought brings me to respect anew my instinct that we as Palestinians are excessively loyal, ordinary, and also godlike. We might even be God's chosen people. We have a duty to exist.

I spent years going back and forth teaching at various UNRWA schools. I don't know why I wasn't able to stay at any one of them for more than a year. When I eventually went to work at one of Lebanon's most exclusive private schools, the looks of surprise and disdain were very obvious on the faces of my acquaintances, colleagues, and even some of my relatives. Lebanese society couldn't understand how a Palestinian could work there without having some connections, and Palestinian society couldn't fathom how a child of Palestine could decline to contribute the fruits of her labor to the offspring of her own people. They conveniently overlooked the fact that the corruption of Palestinian society—if a people living outside of their homeland can be considered a society—and political factionalism had deprived me of a job, even though I had excelled in my studies. As for members of my extended family who asked about the salary, vacations, benefits, and car, none of them seemed to notice that their little girl had obtained a master's degree and published three novels, thus qualifying her to be anywhere, while they were sipping coffee and gossiping about her long absences.

When I observe the fabric of Palestinian society closely, I am often appalled to discover that it's actually threadbare. I recall one episode in particular from my days teaching at UNRWA schools, when another teacher tried to get close to me and I didn't understand what he wanted. I didn't give his attention much thought because I didn't reciprocate his admiration. He was constantly trying to endear himself to me over a period of a couple of months, sometimes flirting with me openly in front of everyone else, in an offensive and repulsive way that just made me nauseous. Apparently, he thought I had a permanent teaching position and when he found out that I was on a daily contract, he stopped saying hello—in fact, after that, I don't even think we saw each other again in the teachers' lounge. This interpretation of events would never have occurred to me had one of my friends not told me that it was well known that he was a bachelor looking for a single woman with a steady job.

Once upon a time, I was idealistic and thought that Palestinians should be pioneers and heroes. I thought that since they had sacrificed their lives for Palestine, materialism wouldn't enslave them. I wanted to believe that we were a people chosen by God to live as demigods or saints.

When I participated in a summer camp for Palestinian children, I realized that we were stuck at the bottom of the glass bottle of life. I couldn't comprehend how the Palestinian organizer, a son of the refugee camp no less, could steal in the name of the children of Palestine and then generously give them the crumbs that resulted from his criminal behavior. I used to assume that pain would bring us together and that those who had suffered as children would certainly want the children of the refugee camps to emerge from their dank and gloomy dwellings. Later, it occurred to me to wonder about Israeli responsibility for some of the crimes perpetrated by Palestinians as a result of their mental pathologies, which they were bound to inherit as a result of the subjugation, denial, and humiliation endured by their forebears. Some years later, I forgave them their pursuit of mendacity as a way of life.

Then the July 2006 War happened. Despite the pain it inflicted and the many sleepless nights it caused, as a Palestinian who had grown tired of hope, I saw it as an opening in the wall of history through which we might escape to Palestine. Interest in the topic of resistance grew, as many drew comparisons with historical Palestinian struggles. The Lebanese resistance forces professed Palestine to be their destination and the liberation of Palestine to be their paramount goal. For me, this talk carried some hope, comfort, or a certain feeling of vindication of my existence. After so many years of Palestinians being denounced and vilified in Lebanon, and deprived of so many basic rights, Palestine and its people in that moment became the destination of all free people in the consciousness of the Arab public. I won't get into the various repercussions and political complications of this consciousness. I just want to bask in the memory of the sweet hopeful feeling it brought me. I began to feel that Palestine was just around the corner: If we say it, it will return, and we will return by our own efforts.

Some of my family actually managed to go back to visit. When both of my paternal uncles experienced kidney failure, my grandfather somehow arranged through the International Red Cross to take them to Palestine for treatment. They came back full of stories about the Israeli doctors and our relatives in Palestine. My grandmother brought back secret supplies of raisins, dried figs, and colorful ceramics, which she stashed away only for us to discover after some insistence. She also kept some soil from Jerusalem, which she dispensed in jars to bless her favorite children and grandchildren. I can vividly recall receiving mine, though at the time I had no concern about how it was acquired and didn't keep a close eye on it at home thereafter.

Much later, my maternal grandmother and my uncle were able to go to Palestine. I remember asking my grandmother Aminah: "Why didn't you stay there, *Teta*?" She cried and wiped her beautiful face with her wrinkled palms. She didn't reply, or maybe she muttered a few words that I didn't understand and didn't bother to try to decipher. But after some time had passed, she told me about the mulberry tree that belonged to her father al-Hajj Mar'i in the village of Mi'ar in northern Palestine. The people of Mi'ar go there every year from their respective exiles, to pick the fruit and be photographed by the cameras of the world.

Khadijeh, My Mother's Mother

INTISAR HAJAJ

(b. Sidon, 1959)

My grandmother Khadijeh and her sewing machine were inseparable twins. Her story began in the village of Qantara in southern Lebanon and unfolded through successive exiles, ending in the refugee camp of 'Ayn al-Hilweh, where she died. She was buried in the nearby city of Sidon, despite her constant entreaties to be buried in her village. She died during the Israeli occupation of southern Lebanon after the invasion of 1982. No one was allowed to return to her village, even in a coffin; the roads were blocked and the checkpoints impassable.

My grandmother Khadijeh, though she lived in Palestine and took refuge in 'Ayn al-Hilweh, never lost her southern Lebanese accent, which was so beautiful and dear to my heart. The south remained in her heart and mind until her death. With every dress she sewed and every stitch she embroidered, she weaved a story of pain, joy, and love. Each thread was spun into a dress of sadness, agony, deprivation, treachery, and incessant migration. My grandmother never ceased to tell her story in detail, especially when she grew old and frail, as though she could restore her youth and beauty by regaling her listeners with the minutest details. I was the youngest grandchild and was enamored with her. I was very influenced by her strong and singular character, as well as her fearlessness. Bravery was in her nature and it guided her behavior. She was very affectionate toward me and my siblings and taught us so many things about life. An expert at sewing, she loved her sewing machine, which became part of her bent frame and animated her once she set to work, overflowing with stories and love. As the machine moved at her command and worked the cloth, her spirit soared over the hills and valleys of southern Lebanon and the plains of the Galilee in Palestine, the memories of her life unfurling before her.

When I sat with her, I was always entranced and excited, curious and inquisitive. I was never happier than when I was cutting cloth for her, handing her needles or spools of thread, or threading the needle. We would sit on the floor and roll out the cloth. Sometimes my mother would help too, since she learned to sew from my grandmother. She had an old-fashioned manual machine. When we sat down, the wheel would make that jarring noise as it began to stitch the cloth, while my grandmother's voice animated her stories. She would continue to create until evening fell, at which point she would finally relax and we would too, before settling down for the night. I loved her stories and her lightheartedness, especially when she was at work, when she didn't hold back and unleashed all the details. I was an attentive and persistent listener, following intently as she told stories about the women of her village and of Palestine, and then relaying them back to her. She'd laugh and say: "It's as if you were there, may you bury me!"

My grandmother Khadijeh's story hasn't ended yet. She repeated her tales to anyone who would listen, to our friends and neighbors in 'Ayn al-Hilweh, until they memorized them, maybe because she sensed the importance of her life story and unrepeatable experiences. She didn't want her memories to disappear and die, as so many people and things had disappeared from her life.

My grandmother loved to drink Arabic coffee with a hand-rolled cigarette. She used only "pure southern tobacco," as she put it, and would sit back and enjoy a few puffs with her morning and evening coffee. She hailed from the beautiful village of al-Qantara, had rosy cheeks until her dying day, and a fair-skinned, well-proportioned body. Her sinewy braid was covered by a white headscarf and her honey-colored eyes radiated intelligence, strength, love, and longing. She was a woman born for love, to love and be loved—and that's how she actually lived. She began her life as the village seamstress, living under the protection of her brother Qasim and his wife, Hajar, who came from Ba'albak and was also their cousin. My grandmother Khadijeh was stubborn and contrary, and that provoked my great-uncle. They would argue until she either left without bending to his will or was beaten by him until she did. She often blamed him for her stomach pains, which started after a blow from his ever-present walking stick. He would laugh it off and say: "That's because you're stubborn, Khadijeh, and won't listen to what I say."

When she was young, she was married to a man from the village for some time but didn't conceive a child. It was a time of massive immigration and the man wanted to discover America, so he immigrated there on the promise that she would follow once he had settled. Two years passed, the man forgot about my grandmother and his village, and then he sent her the divorce papers. She didn't lament his loss too much. She went on with her life, sewing at her machine and helping her brother and his wife plant crops, take care of livestock, and raise children.

Because of the proximity of southern Lebanon and northern Palestine, my grandmother would go regularly to the market in the Palestinian village of al-Khalisa every Tuesday, accompanied by some of her relatives, to buy cloth, thread, and other items. Once she went even farther, to buy a new sewing machine in the town of Safad, which she had ordered in advance from one of the merchants, and that machine still sits in our house in 'Ayn al-Hilweh, awaiting my grandmother's stories. Commerce at the Tuesday market was brisk, and merchants would come from all over Lebanon and Syria to sell their goods and crops. They would stay at the house of the village *mukhtar* or with one of their acquaintances. My grandmother had built up a large group of friends there as a result of her frequent visits and was a dear and valued guest. They loved her and she loved them all. She bought everything she needed there and would return laden with gifts and cloth. But the time she came back with a modern sewing machine, her happiness was indescribable. Her frequent travels to northern Palestine and her love of the people, as well as her sense that there was a demand for a seamstress who could sew and teach others to sew, led her to consider moving there.

My strong grandmother, obstinate and opinionated, never stopped arguing with my great-uncle. He was a few years older than her, but she contended fiercely with him. She compelled him to let her go, but only after she promised that she'd come back during the harvest season and when my great-aunt Hajar was due to give birth. After making many promises, my grandmother took her sewing machine and her essential belongings and set out one morning on the back of a mule, in the company of other travelers from her village. She was tired by the time she got to her destination: the home of the *mukhtar* of al-Khalisa. She was friends with his wife, for whom she made clothes. She told him her story and chose him to be her guardian among all the people whom she loved and who loved her. After a few days as his guest, she found a place to live, settled down, and reveled in her independence. Women began to flock to her, asking her to sew undergarments and other clothes. She got creative with new styles, which made her happy and kept her clients happy too. She was a persuasive talker, but she was also bossy and could impose her ideas, though she always did so with love and without harshness or ridicule. She passed her days between the south and the Galilee, dividing her time between the two places. From time to time, my great-uncle would check up on her to make sure she was well. Then he'd do some shopping and go back to his home village.

In al-Khalisa, my grandmother met 'Isa al-Hamad, a handsome man from a large family who was educated and enlightened. He had been chosen by Kamil al-Husayn, one of the leaders in al-Hula region, to be his companion and right-hand man. She fell in love with 'Isa, and 'Isa became enamored with her. He loved this strange, strong woman above all the women of his village. What magical secrets did this strange woman conceal, which a lover could only discover by setting foot in her land and exploring her landscape? His love for her still echoes among the elderly people of the village who were alive at the time. Despite the opposition of both families to the marriage, it took place after the intervention of the village elders and the acceptance of all my great-uncle's preconditions.

My grandmother married the love of her life and not a day of my life went by without her mentioning him in 'Ayn al-Hilweh, when the memories overflowed from her heart. But she didn't overflow with pining, longing, and love; she exuded anger, hatred, and resentment, for some reason that I, as a little girl, couldn't comprehend. She lived happily with him, she was pampered and ruled as the empress of his heart and life. But, as the saying goes, happiness is never complete, and her happiness wasn't fulfilled because she discovered that she couldn't conceive a child. She visited midwives one by one, and she went to Safad to see doctors, to no avail. Her only concern was to make 'Isa al-Hamad happy and that her heart be gladdened by a child that she bore with him. But her womb remained an infertile field, without sign of so much as a single green sprout. She was beset by sorrow, though she kept trying without success. His family began to pressure him to remarry but he adamantly refused and put his faith in God.

My great-uncle Qasim and great-aunt Hajar had many children, boys and girls, and their last two were beautiful twin girls. Spring blossomed in their faces, the sun's rays mingled with their hair, and green wheat kernels gleamed in their eyes. My grandmother adored those two little girls, Fatima and Maryam, and she reserved a special strange love for Fatima. She yearned for little Fatima whenever they were apart, and cuddled and embraced her whenever they were together. My great-aunt Hajar was carrying a heavy burden. She had a large family and the expanse of land she had to work contained many livestock. The nights were hardly long enough to rest her tired eyes and body. My grandmother Khadijeh used to help her for several days at a time on her many visits. One day, in a flash, it occurred to her that she could take her beloved Fatima, who by this time had weaned and begun to walk, with her to Palestine, where she could raise her as her own daughter. That way, she would lighten the burden on Hajar and become a mother with a little girl who was her flesh and blood. After talking it over with Qasim and Hajar, she got her heart's desire. Maryam stayed with Hajar and Fatima became her aunt Khadijeh's daughter. My grandmother Khadijeh took Fatima and returned to al-Khalisa where she told 'Isa about her desire to adopt her brother's daughter and raise her. 'Isa was delighted and had no objection because of his love for her. 'Isa loved Fatima a great deal and became very attached to her. He hoped that she could be the fair stalk of wheat in a house made of wood.

They played with her and bought her presents and sweets; she got everything she wanted. My grandmother never loved anyone the way she loved Fatima, who stirred her soul and awakened her lifeless womb, enabling her heart to conquer her infertility. Meanwhile, of course, there were regular visits between Fatima and her parents. But despite the happiness that the beautiful, calm Fatima had brought to their lives, 'Isa al-Hamad and his family never gave up on the idea of bringing his own children into the world. The conflict wouldn't come to an end, and my grandmother just wanted to be at peace and to clear her conscience of the burden that continued to weigh on her. So, she stipulated that she would find him a suitable wife herself, someone to live side by side with her so that 'Isa would not leave her sight.

'Isa al-Hamad grudgingly accepted her condition and my grandmother searched for a woman to fit her specifications. Not his. Above all, she sought assurances for herself.

I knew this whole story by heart, having heard it thousands of times under the corrugated metal roof of our house in 'Ayn al-Hilweh refugee camp, where stories were spun over and over during our sewing sessions. As soon as the wheel began to turn, the cabinet of my grandmother's memories would open up. The words didn't stop until the end of her lifetime. We all became caught up in her misfortune and I found myself crying every time I saw tears in her eyes. I worried about all the tears she shed. Her sorrow was incomprehensible to me until I grew older. I learned then that a love killed by one's loved one never expires, is never forgotten, and can't be left behind. Her heart was taken over by loathing and rage, and she never ceased to love her husband, though she denied it frequently. She was most incensed when my mother, Fatima, asked her to forgive and forget, telling her that time had passed and there was no point to all that. She reminded her that displacement and exile were greater than her own personal sorrow and burden. She would say that an entire country had been lost, so she shouldn't be dwelling on her own sorrows, which were better forgotten. This would only make my grandmother irate and she would stop speaking to my mother for several days.

My grandmother chose a wife for her husband, a woman who used to come and sew with her from Hawran, in southern Syria. She was tall, tan, broad, and calm. The woman looked as though she had been born to bear strong, healthy children. My grandmother agreed to the terms with the woman and her parents, with 'Isa's consent, and she arranged for them to be married in the same house. They lived in one room, while she and Fatima lived in the other.

Every time a new life would come into being in the womb of her rival, my grandmother's spirit would agonize and experience great sadness. The fire of jealousy was ignited and conflict simmered between the two women. 'Isa was stuck between two fires, the fire of love and that of father-hood, and it seems that fatherhood won out with the passage of time. The ardor of love abated and the man was overcome by confusion. Finally, he resolved to find a separate house for the wife who was mother of his children, and that was what transpired. The wife chosen by my grandmother above all other women to be her partner had become her enemy. My grandmother's sorrows multiplied, and if it weren't for Fatima, she would have been crushed by her lot in life. 'Isa began to spend most of his time at the other house and my grandmother decided to leave him. My mother, Fatima, was ten years old when Khadijeh decided they would move, pack-ing her belongings against her husband's wishes. They set-tled in the neighboring village, al-Na'ima, which was where my father lived. Khadijeh knew my father's family and went to live among them, and they were very good to her. There, she returned to her sewing machine, sewing to make her liv-ing among good people who embraced her and her daughter.

Fatima grew more and more beautiful over the next few years, as she approached adolescence. My father was a hand-some, tan young man. He was tall, educated, and worked as a teacher in Safad and al-Khalisa. He didn't come home much due to duties at work and the distance to his village. One day he returned to his village at the end of the school day to find a young girl strolling along with the other girls of the village, and he vowed he would marry her. My father introduced himself to her mother, Khadijeh, having heard her story and having gathered that she had a good reputation with his family. My mother, Fatima, was thirteen and my father was twenty-five when he asked for her hand in marriage. My grandmother balked due to her young age and she consulted her own family in the village, who objected strongly. But my father insisted and offered a large dowry befitting the beautiful girl. After some give and take, including the intervention of the village elders, he got what he wanted. In 1946, my father married my mother, Fatima, daughter of Khadijeh, and daughter of Hajar and Qasim, and they lived in the same neighborhood as his parents. My father's mother wasn't happy that he had married the outsider, since, according to her, the girls in his extended family were more worthy. However, my father's resolve and his great love for Fatima caused him to circumvent his mother's objections, along with the customs and rituals of the era.

My father loved Fatima, who was his darling wife and his precious favorite. He called her "flower of the south" and they spent a beautiful year together, amidst the green meadows and clear ponds, where they would go fishing. Toward the end of 1947, at fourteen years old, my mother gave birth to my eldest brother in al-Na'ima. He was only a few months old when the Zionist Haganah forces attacked the villages of the Galilee and massacred the civilian populations, precipitating mass migration from the region. They left in a hurry, gathering some belongings and departing as one large clan, led by the elders toward south Lebanon. They went on foot and left behind their thriving houses and precious livestock. They left their paradise and walked all night toward my mother's village, al-Qantara. They arrived at dawn overwhelmed by fear, hunger, and exhaustion. They lived there for some time among relatives, but my father's family was divided: some wanted to remain in Lebanon while others preferred to go to Syria, where they planned to make war against the Israelis and regain their land. But my father didn't want to venture farther; they would stay with the house keys at the ready for whenever they heard of some victory here or battle there.

In the beginning, the promise was that they would return in a mere ten days, but the days stretched into years, and the keys remained without doors. Guests are burdensome in every time and place, no less so when those guests are a large family staying with their extended family, just waiting to go home. The villagers of al-Qantara were exceptionally gracious and hospitable to them. My great-uncle Qasim, in particular, was very solicitous, but after a few months my father was fed up and decided to follow other family members who had settled in various other parts of Lebanon. At that time, the United Nations Relief and Works Agency (UNRWA) had begun assisting people and finding temporary shelters for them until things were settled. My father decided they should migrate to the town of Nabatiyeh, so my grandmother gathered their things together and they all left. The extended family split up and spread out, settling in different areas of south Lebanon. My father rented a stone house in the village of Kfar Rumman, which is still standing today. My father was an educated man, who knew English as a result of having done compulsory service in the British army before he had become a schoolteacher in al-Khalisa. He applied for a job at UNRWA and worked there distributing food rations, also known as "subsistence rations," to the refugees living in the camp of Nabatiyeh.

In Kfar Rumman my mother, now sixteen, had a daughter. If my grandmother had not been with her constantly, she would not have been able to carry that burden. Life became harder, people were dispersed; they walked the streets and slept in the orchards under olive trees. Life was catastrophically upended for a people who had been living peaceably in their homeland. They suddenly found themselves homeless. Whose wrath had they incurred to deserve such a fate? Without work, people would congregate anywhere there was an old wooden radio to follow developments in Palestine and to hear about the prospects for return, a return that they continue to await.

After a couple of years, many refugees had gathered near Sidon, and my father decided to join them. He left his job, packed his belongings, and went with his family and some relatives to the eternal capital of refuge, 'Ayn al-Hilweh. Tents had been pitched there in a flat area surrounded by small hills and lemon orchards. The tents were arrayed in neat rows, like ghosts floating in the air with feet planted in the ground, their corners fixed with rocks. These ghosts just added to the nightmares that have haunted those families ever since. Most tents sheltered more than one family; refugees had no privacy. A refugee is just barely a human being. There was nothing they could do. A refugee is a human without rights, destined to wait. Everyone surrendered to the sight of a country being swallowed up before their eyes, waiting for the Arabs to be victorious, just waiting for a miracle, and they've been waiting ever since the Nakba. At that point, my mother was pregnant with her third child.

In early September 1951, heavy rains fell and flooded the camp, including my mother's tent, where she had just had her third child. Everything was afloat, including the foam mattress, and people rushed to help my mother, grandmother, and the three children. My mother and grandmother never forgot those exceedingly difficult days. A few months later, 'Ayn al-Hilweh began to be built up with small houses with corrugated metal roofs. My father rented a wooden shed that consisted of one large room, where my mother bore three more children. Several years later, he built a house of stone in another neighborhood and the large family moved there. My father's burdens had increased, and he found himself in straitened circumstances as the Nakba went on, so he decided to travel to Saudi Arabia to work as a teacher. That was in 1958. The growing family was left in the charge of my grandmother and mother, two mothers who raised the children and presided over the household. My grandmother now had her own room in a house consisting of three bedrooms, a kitchen, and a bathroom. She resumed her sewing and built up a new set of customers. In addition to her household duties, my grandmother Khadijeh used to compete with my mother in playing the maternal role. She intervened in every detail, large and small, to the point that she even named most of the children.

The camp is a small space, constructed in a hurry by people from all over Palestine, and its neighborhoods came to be called after the names of towns and villages in Palestine. The camp knows nothing of urban planning—the term doesn't even appear in its lexicon. The people in the camp are united by the fact that they are all treated indiscriminately, as though they lacked faces and names, or as though a special law had been made for them alone among all humans. Winter for them has a song of its own that isn't heard anywhere else. In summer, the heat overpowers the human bodies crammed together in overcrowded rooms under corrugated metal roofs, which are usually riddled with holes. As soon as your feet touch the threshold of the house in the morning you're greeted by the odious stench of the sewers. Narrow alleys, winding roads, twisty paths, dirty in the summer and muddy in the winter, making plastic boots your constant companion. Yet, joy and contentment were present in our lives. We thought that the camp was our eternal world and didn't complain much or aspire to anything more, as long as we were surrounded by kind faces that smiled despite the adversity and harshness of life.

The houses around us multiplied and we came to have neighbors from a variety of Palestinian towns and villages. It was a fortunate coincidence that one of the distinctive features of our neighborhood was that it included many women from south Lebanon who were married to Palestinian men. That was a great source of comfort to my mother and grandmother. They were indescribably glad to have neighbors like Umm Musa Faydah from Mays al-Jabal and Umm Salah Nahla Mansur from 'Aynatha. But the woman closest to my mother's heart was Umm Musa al-Ghul, who was my grandmother's good friend and close to her in age. During their visits, around cups of coffee and hand-rolled cigarettes, they would tell stories about their lives, from their villages to the camp. In 'Ayn al-Hilweh, the south was always in our house, and Palestine was always present in south Lebanon. We were proud of this hybrid, in the midst of a community that was predominantly Palestinian, and we never felt any difference between those who came from over here and those who hailed from over there. Our neighborhood also had Syrians, Kurds, Jordanians, and others; it was a joyous mixture from all over the Levant joined together in a space called a camp.

Taking responsibility for six children in the absence of their father was a tall order. My mother had to be affectionate and stern at one and the same time. Our only contact with our father was by means of the mail. Letters would arrive at the shop of Abu Kamil al-Safsaf in the lower main road of the camp that led to our house. We could hardly contain our happiness when my grandmother or one of my siblings arrived with a letter from him. We would gather around to listen to my father's news and hear about his longing for my mother and for us. Since my father would return once a year in the 1960s, my mother had two more children, for a total of eight: four boys and four girls.

My grandmother kept her sewing machine in her bedroom. As her customers increased, her stories spread ever farther, to listeners from other neighborhoods. She sewed, darned, and mended clothes, both new and tattered, sealing up the holes so that they could be worn again. My grandmother never grumbled and worked for meagre coins but didn't haggle. As the years passed, more seamstresses began to appear in other neighborhoods and my grandmother's customers decreased, but the poorest of them kept coming because they could afford her despite their limited means.

As for 'Isa al-Hamad, he settled with his family in the refugee camp of Nabatiyeh, making his living by running a grocery store. He regretted having abandoned my grandmother, who would gather his news from his sister who came to visit her from time to time in 'Ayn al-Hilweh. My grandmother never tried to see him; she was content to hear his news secondhand. Nor did he try to see her, as though the love and passion had dried up forever. 'Isa was preoccupied with his own family's concerns, living with a woman whom he never loved, and minding a store where he received no visitors. My mother tells us that she never understood why my grandmother left her husband, despite knowing the familiar story. She couldn't grasp how she managed to put that great love behind her. It was as though she had poured concrete over her heart and it had turned to stone.

But in truth my grandmother never recovered from the anguish of separation and rejection, and she constantly prayed that he would die before her. She often reminisced about the days of happiness and plenty in Palestine and griped about life in the camp and its miseries, in spite of her strong affection for it. In 1974 'Isa al-Hamad was killed when Nabatiyeh refugee camp was destroyed in its entirety in an Israeli attack. My grandmother had no reaction; she didn't even shed a tear, at least not that we saw. She remained silent and kept to her room until the following day.

My shy, discreet, beautiful mother was my grandmother's jewel and ours too. She loved my father deeply. She was brought up by him from the time she was a child and learned many things from him, such as the love of poetry and knowledge, even though she couldn't read or write. She loved to listen to Fairuz in the morning and Umm Kulthum and 'Abdul Wahab at night, and we imbibed her aesthetic taste. Sometimes she would get carried away by the music and sing along with her warm voice that expressed emotions older than her youthful age. My mother is a reasonable woman, with a transparent soul like a clear spring of water.

She was also a dutiful wife to an absent husband and resisted being swept up by my grandmother's strong will, which she imposed imperiously every step of the way. That led to many conflicts between them, which could end in several days of estrangement before relations were eventually restored. My grandmother was strongly attached to my mother and couldn't endure a long rift. Their love was always imbued with peace and forgiveness, as it should be between mother and daughter.

We all grew older, my grandmother and mother included, and my father aged alone in the distant desert. He would visit us only in the summer, the rest of the year only being in touch through letters. This went on until 1981, when he finally decided to return to Lebanon, ending twenty-five years of scorching exile. For these twenty-five years he didn't see us grow in front of his eyes, his only means of seeing us being the black-and-white photos we sent him. Meanwhile, my mother spent her life in the exile of the refugee camp, like a fresh flower with petals surrounding its stem, dreaming of the summer. She was content with her lot and felt grateful for the presence of my grandmother, who was her biggest helper. We were well-off relative to the other camp dwellers, with most men in the camp doing agricultural work in the orchards of Sidon and its vicinity.

My grandmother witnessed all of Israel's wars from the Nakba to the Israeli invasion of 1982. She grew frail and her eyesight and hearing weakened, so that sewing eventually became too difficult. Full of regrets, she retired and passed her sewing machine on to my mother. The mirror became her only friend. She would talk to it, tug on her sagging cheeks, and lament her lost beauty. She would touch her fingers to her lips, which were no longer able to hold a cigarette, then slap her infirm thighs and say: "Is this what's become of you, Khadijeh? Alas!" My sisters and I would listen and tease her, saying that her beauty was long gone, and she would respond testily with curses: "When I was blossoming in my prime, where were you, you brute?" Then we'd all giggle loudly and hug her, apologizing for our obnoxiousness. Time seems to take people by surprise. They wake up one day to find that old age has overtaken them faster than the wind.

As for us, life led us down various paths in different directions, while my grandmother remained with my mother and father in the camp. At 103 years old, unable to stand on her own, she seemed diminutive and childlike. At the end, she abstained from food and drink and asked frequently about the village, her family, and about each one of us. One day in March 1986, she released her soul while lying alone in bed, far from the soil of her birthplace, which had nurtured her like a majestic oak tree, and where she had wanted to be buried. She was as giving as the fig tree that she had brought from al-Qantara and transplanted to our house in 'Ayn al-Hilweh.

And the Dream Goes On

RUBA RAHME

(b. Damascus, 1986)

Yearning overcomes me every night before I sleep.

When I close my eyes, I feel her small hands touching my cheek. I wish I could hug her one last time and feel her curly hair, which is so soft to the touch.

The walls of our house long for her laughter and her gentle footsteps, amidst all the dreadful memories that haunt us. Her toys are still strewn around the floor. I'm loath to pick them up in case my memories of her vanish.

They've lain there ever since she left. Maybe in Germany she'll get to know her father, who left her when she was only six months old. Maybe it's time that they met.

My mother left one year ago for Holland, and my father three years ago to Turkey and then Greece, my brothers following him. So I became mother and father to my brother Salih and my sister Hazar, who stayed with me here in Lebanon. And I became a grandmother to Farah, Hazar's daughter, who made me happy every time I came home. She would hug me and tell me long stories about what happened that day, stories I couldn't understand. She used to ask me about Bilal ("Dal") and *Khalo* Salih ("Halo Talih") and our conversation would always end like this:

"OK, Buba (Ruba)!"

"OK, apple of Buba's eye."

"Buba, I wub (love) you."

I love you too. You were the joy of the entire household. When you arrived, we couldn't decide on a name for you, but when your grandmother chose your name, everyone was persuaded.

"We'll call her 'Farah' (joy)—maybe joy will return to this household."

You were right, mother, but you couldn't have foreseen that when she left, she would steal the joy away from our hearts once and for all.

I wasn't sure she'd remember me after she left, but her German doctor told my sister Hazar that her sudden wake-ups during the night were due to psychological trauma from being separated from me and Salih. How surprising that a girl scarcely older than two could know the meaning of love and yearning. But maybe not. She used to call me "Mama," since I was her second mother. Mothers aren't just the ones who give birth but also those who nurture and love; a mother's sister is a half-mother.

Farah was my little girl, whose every day I observed. I noticed when she began to walk, her mischievousness, the way she disturbed my papers. She imitated my every move: how I sat or held my cell phone. My sister woke up so many times at night terrified to find her child's bed empty, only to find her lying in mine. I wouldn't have believed her if she hadn't sent me a picture that makes me tear up whenever I look at it: a tiny body sleeping soundly on top of my blanket. I never felt her weight because I was always in a deep sleep after a long day of strenuous work.

Her birth was a source of joy at a time when sadness had enveloped the household after my brother-in-law, her father, had been imprisoned. In her ninth month my sister Hazar lost her husband, who couldn't be there with her when she gave birth.

When she came, we had a long list of names for her, but my mother's choice made us all realize that that's what we needed in our family. Farah is her name and with her arrival joys started pouring into our household. When she was two months old, her father was released and met her for the first time and was able to embrace his wife again. While he was imprisoned, my sister never stopped looking for some means to legalize his status and to have her childbirth recognized on Lebanese soil. The never-ending complications to register new births were among the worst bureaucratic hurdles for Palestinian and Syrian refugees in Lebanon.

Farah lived with both parents for less than a year before her father could no longer bear the humiliation. His official documents had been stamped with the word "Departure" and that constituted a constant threat to his presence in Lebanon. So he decided to leave westward by sea with the aim of going to Germany. When Hazar said goodbye to him she didn't know if they would ever meet again, so she resigned herself to being both mother and father again.

When Farah was a year and a half old my mother also left by sea, leaving the three of us with the little girl. Farah hugged me every night before going to sleep and imprinted a wet kiss on my cheek. Her fingers told me that I was the dearest to her heart and that she would transport me with her childish dreams to a place of eternal happiness.

Once, I was away from home for five days, and every day, her mother told me, Farah would stand at the door of our house and cry out, "Buba, oh Buba!" On my return, when I opened the door of the house, she saw me and started to cry and shout in a very bizarre way. She approached me, hugged me, then turned away. She placed her tiny hands on my face and hugged me again, crying ceaselessly. She had never welcomed me with tears before.

After we celebrated her second birthday, there was some movement on Hazar's family reunification application, and one day she announced that she had been granted an appointment at the German embassy. I told her that I didn't like it when she pulled my leg. But several days later she showed me her travel document and Farah's passport with the visas stamped inside them. I looked closely to make sure it was true and not another bad joke.

The countdown began for a new departure. Every night I looked out at the stars from my balcony. I would count them carefully, but each time I would make a mistake and a monstrous airplane would take shape before my eyes. It would crash into my body and tear me into shreds as it transported my loved ones to a place where I could see them only through a phone screen, depending on the speed of the internet connection and its vagaries.

I said goodbye so many times that I worried that there would be no one left to say goodbye to me. I thought that I would get used to their absence after a while, as was my habit, but Farah lived in the nooks of the house, her scent lingered in the corners, and her innocent voice continued to ring in my ears: "Buba, come here."

After they left, Salih and I no longer had Hazar to ask after us, in her maternal way, whenever we were late coming back home. And we had to take on the responsibilities of cooking and housework. It was generally accepted that she was strong and could always take care of herself. But she

was constantly evading the bad luck that dogged her and the
envious eyes that followed her, a smile ever-present on her
face as if to indicate that good times were always ahead.

She was my friend before she was my sister, maybe
because she was the family member with whom I lived long-
est, and we rarely quarreled or fought as siblings do. She
could tell what I was thinking before I said a word.

After Salih and I returned from the airport, I went to
my closet to change my clothes and found that she had covered the inside of the door with stickers on which she'd written the various pieces of advice she often gave me: "Take
care of yourself," "Don't be late," "Be patient with your
brother Salih."

I don't know what divine wisdom arranged for me to
remain alone with my youngest brother, Salih, who was then
nineteen. He was fond of karate and break dancing, but his
acrobatics and walking on walls made me worry about him.
At the same time, I was proud of him because he always
stood out among his peers. He'd been the ringleader of the
kids in our neighborhood ever since he was a child, when we
lived in Yarmuk refugee camp in Syria. He'd made money by
selling cactus fruit, candied apples, and milk pudding made
by my mother, advertising his wares by calling out in a loud
voice through the neighborhood. Sometimes, our neighbor
'Abla would hear him and buy the whole batch, and he would
return with a smile on his small face. He used to make the
most of my aunt's presence during summer vacations, when
she would visit from the Emirates. She would offer him
an enticing sum for the whole lot, but his childlike morals
would compel him to return the correct change with a shy
smile. Then she'd insist that she wasn't taking it, leaving him

with a large profit for the day. In the evenings, he would count his earnings and get ready for the following day.

Once, my father went to check on a supply of aluminum sheeting that he was storing in my late grandfather's house, only to discover that his insolent son had arranged to sell some of it for less than five Syrian pounds.

Salih wasn't a spoiled youngest child. My eldest brother was the one most indulged by my father, especially since he had come after four girls. Salih was the defiant one who wouldn't rest until he got what he wanted by whatever means.

When Salih was a little older, he made my parents promise that if he graduated from intermediate school, they would get him his own computer. But as soon as Salih graduated and was getting ready to enter secondary school, the war in Syria began.

Once we reached Lebanon, it wasn't easy for him to continue his schooling because the supporting documents that he needed to enroll were elusive and the curriculum was in English rather than Arabic.

Despair began to set in for the boy, barely fifteen, who scarcely knew what had happened to him. He didn't understand why he had to start looking for a job while other boys of his age had smartphones and nice clothes and were playing pranks on their teachers. To make matters worse, his parents abandoned him in the bloom of youth, one after the other. He never got his computer.

Sometimes I think I hear him yawning when I wake up in the middle of the night, but I get up only to find that he's crying. I go back to bed agonizing over what has happened to us. My mother's decision to emigrate to Holland, braving the sea, wilderness, and other dangers, was taken mainly for his sake.

After Hazar left, he stayed in bed for three days, mourning her loss. I stifled my sadness and made him think that I was happy for her. But I cried in secret for our loss of a second loving mother.

Salih also began to have erratic ideas that confused and jarred me. One day he would say that he wanted a tattoo on his chest, and the next that he wanted to adopt a dog. Sometimes he would discover that he was a communist at heart, and at other times he would report that he was embracing Islam. Then he would tell me he was going back to Syria, or accuse me of failing him, or of caring more about my students than about him. Often, he would show great remorse over his behavior and resolve that it was his duty, not mine, to be the main income earner. Then he would show up with a broken foot or nose or other bodily injury from playing football.

I generally remained silent in these situations. I'd just stand there, flabbergasted at his behavior and his unrealistic expectations. Then I would retire to my room to gather my composure, before returning with carefully chosen words to preserve what remained of my family.

In fact, there was no one I loved more than him and I tried as much as I could to get him everything he desired. But his unruly behavior made me resent my father for leaving us behind and abandoning us. At the same time, I felt as though God knew that I was the one most tolerant of his immature adolescence.

When I heard his voice reciting the Qur'an while praying, it reminded me of the voice of my father, who always urged us not to neglect our prayers, especially the dawn prayer. In Yarmuk camp, he would lead us in prayer by reciting the *sura* of the Cave or Yasin from the Qur'an, while we contended with the chill of the ablution water in winter. We didn't really understand the meaning of piety then—not until we were older. We would remain quiet and look over at our mother, who had memorized all the verses.

Our house had been warm in winter, thanks to the kerosene heater in the middle of the living room. The family would gather around it, my father, mother, five girls, and two boys, and the aroma of toasted bread would mingle with that of roasted onions. My father's rich voice would break out in song and we would giggle when our parents competed over who was more popular with the opposite sex in their youth. We always took my mother's side, since my father usually managed to make her jealous. But he'd always end by exclaiming, "Come, my bride, do you think that I could live without you?"

My father still thinks about his shop, which was so well located with its two entrances, one on the main street of Yarmuk camp and the other opening out onto our neighborhood, the Fida'iyin Quarter. He had meticulously chosen the style of the tiles and had handpicked his employees. The range of pastries and ice-cream flavors were carefully chosen to attract customers. It gladdened his heart, after twenty years of travel, toil, and drudgery, to be able to set up his own business.

It had only been in operation for a year and a half when fear began to infiltrate the depths of the camp and my father left for Beirut, taking my brother Muhammad with him to spare him compulsory military service. No doubt, he thinks that his shop is still standing. We always prayed that he wouldn't see the clips on YouTube that showed it completely destroyed. Maybe he knows, but we humans have the capacity to live off the remnants of hope.

Yarmuk camp wasn't an ordinary camp like 'Ayn al-Hilweh or the other refugee camps in Lebanon. It was a city with impressive buildings and wide streets. All the main stores in Damascus, even the most renowned and oldest establishments, had branches in Yarmuk.

Yarmuk was a safe haven for Palestinians, as well as for a good number of Syrians, though no one ever asked whether you were Syrian or Palestinian, Sunni or 'Alawi.

The words that united the residents of Yarmuk were "brother" and "sister" and we all worked as one. At the beginning of the Syrian events, many people tried to get the Palestinians involved in the mayhem, as our parents tell it. But we young people kept our opinions to ourselves, not out of fear, but to preserve our dignity amidst the gossip and accusations from evildoers. That's how things remained until the day of our second Nakba, December 16, 2012, when warplanes of the Syrian regime bombed the Mosque of 'Abdul Qadir al-Husayni, and we started talking about evacuating the camp in anticipation of another bombing.

I wasn't there at the time of the bombing. I was in the Mezzeh quarter of Damascus completing my first day at a hairdressing training course. We heard the news about the assault on the camp and hurried back. When we arrived, it was a shock to see the area known as Watermelon Square crowded like the day of judgment. The side adjoining the camp was eerily empty. I rushed in that direction, but a rifle blocked my path and someone shouted at me:

"Where to?"

"I want to go home; I need to see my family."

"Can't you see that the street is being shot at? We're here to protect you."

"What are you talking about? Protect us? I need to enter the camp."

The soldiers' orders were to allow no one to cross the square into the camp, but all I could think of was my mother's voice and the cries of my siblings. I pushed the rifle out of the way and walked ahead, and soon noticed that one of the soldiers was trailing me. He ordered me to run past the deserted area to get to my neighborhood on the other side. There, we met a neighbor, who stopped the soldier from entering our neighborhood, so as not to give the opposition a pretext to enter from the other side. The people of our quarter tried to remain neutral.

I found my mother as I imagined her. I kissed her hands, and when I lifted my eyes to meet hers, she told me that my cousins had insisted that we leave our apartment. But her response had been reminiscent of my late grandfather Abu 'Ali's: "The biggest mistake we made in our lives was to leave Palestine, on the grounds that we'd be back in a few days. And here we remain, since 1948. Those few days are yet to end."

We had no choice but to leave. Yarmuk was held in captivity like Gaza, and Israel lived in the hearts of the evildoers there. My camp was splintered into fragments and our childhood stories were scattered everywhere.

Every day I wake up in Sidon dreaming of Yarmuk and of my mother going about her daily chores after returning from work at the elementary school, as though the war had never occurred and the walls of our house had not been demolished. I go back to sleep hoping not to wake up. For I wake up only to find that the houses we live in are not ours. They belong to people who demand rent, electricity charges, and water fees at the start of each month. I need to work to pay even for the air that I breathe.

Lebanon is the only country to admit Palestinians from Syria, although under Lebanese law we are recognized neither as Palestinian refugees nor as Syrians. We are not residents, but nor are we tourists, refugees, nor even migrants; we are some special category, as checkpoint officials choose to remind us frequently.

"What's your name?"

"Ruba."

"Where are you from, Ruba?"

"From Tiberias."

"How come you say you're from Tiberias, yet it says here: Damascus?"

"Sorry, but you asked me where I was from, and I answered."

"So, you mean you're not satisfied with Syria, which did you a favor and took you in all those years ago?"

We weren't condescending to the Lebanese when they came to Damascus during their civil war. We shared our homes and blankets and divided the relief tasks among ourselves to help them. Now the tables have turned and we're the ones who are displaced, our lives gone awry.

What are we supposed to dream about now? Should I dream of a return to Syria and Yarmuk camp? Or to Tiberias, which I've only seen reflected in the tears of my grandfather? Or should I dream of emigration across the sea to Europe, where my family is now?

When I express my fears and sorrows to the sea, it becomes enraged and beckons me to dive into it and escape. But I deflect its efforts to entice me. I recount the stories about the smugglers who traffic in people; the children, mothers, and fathers who drown in the merciless sea. Then I recall that the sea took pity on my mother and brother, refraining from swallowing them up when they made their way to Holland by way of Turkey. Sometimes I thank the sea or cry in its lap, and it splatters its waves on my face so that no one can see my tears.

I think of my grandfather, Abu 'Ali al-Tabrani, who when I was young would fold me into the blanket that covered his back and shoulders so that my small head would poke out. He told me stories about the net that he used to fish with in Lake Tiberias and showed me the key to his house in Palestine. He would laugh when he told me how my grandmother gave birth to my father in Hawran in Syria after they were displaced from Palestine in 1948. He gave me some of his old photographs, saying: "Keep these pictures so that when I die, you'll remember me. I'm going to give your mother the key, my prayer beads, and my small penknife, so that when you return to Palestine you'll be prepared. They'll be safest with her."

I took the photos and ran up the stairs to our house on the second floor, excited to tell my mother what he had just confided. But it just made her angry, and she made me go back downstairs and tell him: "May you live a long life, *jiddi*."

I never knew what death meant until I lost him. I would ask my mother when he would return, and she would respond only by crying and hugging me silently.

Time passes quickly and the sea and I start talking about the land beyond the mountains, where our departed loved ones have gone, and now the sun is also announcing its departure.

The sunset gladdens my heart and the sparkling threads of light on the surface of the water show me that there's beauty in life and that after every setting sun, sorrow, and yearning, there's hope, love, and a new encounter.

* * *

My sister Salam had a tendency to rebel against reality, and noticing it I felt enamored of our Palestinian-ness. At eighteen, she filled our house in 'Ayn al-Hilweh with children from the camp and taught them how to dance *dabkeh* to Palestinian tunes. I was full of wonder at her loving eyes and her stirring voice.

These were the beginnings of the Laji' (Refugee) performing arts group, whose first show left the audience in tears. When Salam recited the poem "Visa," she motioned toward each of the distinguished guests in the first row. I couldn't restrain myself from crying too, I was so moved by her reproach of our political officials.

At secondary school in Syria, Salam had devised ways of solving math problems that astonished her teachers. Her ambition then was to study atomic or high-energy physics at university. But when she got to Lebanon, tears and depression became her constant companions, until it was time for her to leave by sea.

She wasn't like the character she played on stage, Umm Talal, who said goodbye to her son Talal before he died at sea. She was stronger, and she made it to Holland in 2015 without ever giving up.

At that time, I was teaching the Syrian school curriculum to the third intermediate and secondary classes. The students would go to Syria to take the official exams, then return to their families in Lebanon. But sometimes their luck would run out and they would get stuck between the Syrian and Lebanese borders at al-Masna'—just because they were Palestinian. So they were forced to work at the mercy of tyrants, for daily wages not exceeding ten thousand Lebanese liras, or around seven US dollars.

Bilal was one of the children who was stuck. He couldn't return to Syria to take the exam, so he worked for his father in construction in Lebanon. He'd wait for me every day, his clothes splattered with plaster and covered in dust, with sweat drenching his tan face, and his eyes sparkling with joy when I walked past the construction site where he worked.

He was fourteen when I taught him Arabic. He loved me as students sometimes love their teachers. Knowing what adolescents are like, I always chose my words carefully with my students, but I couldn't resist openly expressing my affection for Bilal.

He introduced me to his whole family, and his sister became a close friend of mine. He even started calling me "Mama." I was thrilled to feel as though I had a loving, obedient child, but it alarmed me that he didn't take his mother's feelings into account, though she just laughed it off.

Bilal volunteered to help with *dabkeh* training after Salam left, as he was very skilled in movement and choreography.

The group's numbers grew, comprising Syrians and Lebanese as well as Palestinians, and we soon had separate trainers for theater, *dabkeh*, break dance, and singing. We began to gain fame performing shows all over Lebanon. Laji' became my family after my real family had immigrated, consuming all my time and love. I became a mother to every member of the group, especially Bilal.

When Bilal left his construction job, we thought hard about how he could resume his education after a hiatus of two years. The technical school in Sidon was the only option, since it accepted all students, even Palestinians. He now puts on a school uniform, carries a backpack, and, like all students, complains about getting up early and celebrates on holidays. When I go to pick him up from school he brags to his friends about his young new mom. I'm delighted when his teachers tell me how well-behaved he is in class and how he's excelling academically.

One of the hardest wars we fought was the war to break free of the past, to find ourselves a place of joy, to separate from a world in which the right of return was imagined to be inside a box of rations, to act out—albeit on a stage—our rapidly evaporating dreams.

No one can appreciate the ties that bind unless they've tasted what it's like to have a family that takes care of you, reveling in your joys and lamenting your sorrows. They worry about me walking alone at night along the coastal road after an evening of training, they introduce me to their mothers and sisters, they celebrate one another's birthdays with surprises. They bicker and quarrel, but then they make up with loving messages on WhatsApp, and we all bask in the glow of reconciliation.

I remain certain that I'll see my family again, but I've become a mother to others who are now a part of me. How could I leave them, as my mother left me? How is a mother to leave her children, her darlings, to return to the misery of 'Ayn al-Hilweh, or the tyranny of employers, or the gossip of villains, or a life of loitering in cafés?

Because we're refugees, we need to endure. We need to avoid roads with Lebanese military checkpoints that never stop demanding that we renew our residency permits. So I submit my documents and pay the $200 fee for a three-month extension of residency, but the application is rejected. Mockingly, they tell me to leave Lebanon and return to Syria.

How can I go back? The last time I visited Syria, in 2013, I was so eager to leave.

I should have listened to my parents and stayed with them in Lebanon, but I returned with Hazar to our great paradise, Syria, and took in the scent of our house in Yarmuk, the sight of rubble strewn all over the streets, and the new checkpoint erected by the Syrian regime to monitor the entrance of the camp. Our old neighborhood had become a flashpoint in the conflict between the regime and the opposition, but still we lined up in the long queue to enter the camp. Before it was our turn to enter, an elderly woman whispered in my ear: "Would you carry a bag of bread for me, my dear?" The military checkpoint prevented anyone from taking in more than a single bag of bread.

We couldn't get to our house along the old route from the main entrance, but we managed to approach from the far end. Severed electricity lines were strewn about on the ground and damaged water cisterns were leaking out onto the walls, pockmarked with bullet holes. At one point, I turned around to confront a man whose face was entirely covered apart from two glowering eyes, pointing a rifle toward me.

"Your identity card. What are you doing here?"

"Who are you? I'm going to my house."

"You can't go in, the area is dangerous. Go back where you came from."

The fighting had started again, and it wasn't going to stop for us.

A child of no more than fifteen carrying a rifle that was almost taller than he was led us through narrow streets to Palestine Street, which was echoing to the sounds of armed clashes and the shrieks of sniper fire. The body of an elderly man lay in the street.

We ducked behind a refrigerator containing soda bottles. There we met a woman in her thirties wearing stiletto high-heeled shoes and an expression of fear—but not of death; it was of something else she was hiding.

Why was she dressed so strangely? She held my hand tightly, but Hazar was not so keen on her accompanying us. "Would it be all right for you to take your shoes off and run?" "No, I can't, the ground is covered with glass and metal." "OK, we'll count to three and make a run for it." With moments separating us from death, we held each other's hands tight, recited the Islamic *shahada*, and ran.

I left that woman in the middle of the street because she was moving so slowly in her shoes. My sister was right: why should I die to save that bizarrely dressed woman? But we waited for her before making the final crossing to the side of life.

We fell silent after we emerged from the camp. Our hearts were heavy with the sight of dead bodies on the ground, the holes in the walls of our houses, and the broken stem of a jasmine bush lying in the middle of the street.

On the day we were to leave Syria, we stood in line at the exit point at the border. Hazar was right in front of me, and I watched as her passport received the exit stamp. Then it was my turn. I handed my passport to the border official and he pressed some keys on his computer. Then he looked up with a worried expression and asked me to wait where I stood. That prompted me to contact one of my relatives and give him my location. As he was preparing to come to my aid, I told my sister to take all my belongings and go to Lebanon, so that my mother wouldn't lose two daughters at once. As we were arguing, the soldier returned and asked me to accompany him. He led me behind the counter to a room teeming with men with fierce expressions on their faces and stars on their shoulders.

I gathered up the courage to ask him why I was being detained and was startled by sneering laughter from behind me. A large, square-faced ogre with bloodshot eyes growled: "Your sentence is death!"

Overwhelmed, I collapsed on the bench behind me. At that moment a strong blow reverberated through the room and landed on the face of an elegantly dressed, pale young man. He looked about twenty years old, and his clothes suggested an affluent lifestyle.

"How dare you chew gum in my presence! Throw it out now!"

"Yessir."

"Are you dealing drugs at university?"

"What, me?"

"Yes, you."

The exchange didn't go on much longer. They put his few personal belongings in a brown envelope, took his luggage, and recorded his personal details. I lost track of what happened next because a uniformed young man had just opened a large folder next to me. He found what he was looking for and started interrogating me:

"Where were you living?"

"In the Yarmuk camp."

"And after you left, where did you go?"

"To my aunt's house in Damascus."

"What were you doing?"

"I was a university student."

"Have you ever been to Ma'adamiyya?"

"No, I haven't, I don't even know where that is."

As my fears began to escalate, I heard him murmur to the ogre, "It seems she's not the one we're looking for."

An hour passed during which I felt as though the venom of a snake was slowly infiltrating every vein in my body. I couldn't think of anything but my mother and how she would receive the news.

My train of thought was interrupted by the sound of Hazar shouting at the soldiers. She was demanding to be let in to see me and to talk to the officer in charge.

My sister the troublemaker; she wouldn't leave me even when I asked her to. The ogre told them to let her in and she then had the temerity to ask him to speak to our relative on the phone, who had good connections in the Syrian regime. She smiled at me as if to assure me of her protection, even though she was three years younger. Her courage made me tearful as I waited for the ogre to take the phone. Instead, his tone changed as he replied to her:

"I don't talk to anyone in an unofficial capacity. Anyway, I'm going to release her in half an hour."

Then he turned to me: "Come here." He said: "Did we hit you?"

"No."

"Did we touch you?"

"No."

"So why are you crying? Are we so scary? Ha!"

The soldier who had interrogated me then gave me a scrap of paper on which was written a long number, a date, and the instruction: "Refer to Division of Political Security, Damascus outskirts."

I made sure that my sister crossed the Syrian border, giving her my luggage and promising that I would follow in a matter of days. I stood and watched the bus carrying her away to Lebanon, before returning to my aunt's house. Would I really go to that division to figure out why they were preventing me from leaving?

For the next three months I was holed up in my aunt's house. Eventually, I got sick of hearing: "They've got nothing on you. It's just a matter of someone with a similar name. But don't go to inquire, no one leaves that place."

The house was designed in the traditional Arabic style, with rooms surrounding a central hall. From that time, I recall the aroma of jasmine flowers, the cat that would clamber in every day to explore the empty rooms, the plaintive strains of songs about distant lovers, and, every night, my never-ending tears. I would hear my aunt's footsteps climbing the stairs to my room, coming to embrace me and reassure me that I would soon be reunited with my family.

One day, I got tired of hiding and decided to venture out to discover what they were charging me with. Somehow, without my telling her, my mother must have known, for she unexpectedly contacted me. She asked me to turn back and to be patient until there was some opening. Shortly afterward, my parents sent me some money with a taxi driver, who also gave me two oranges that he had brought for his family. He asked if there was anything I needed from Lebanon. I teared up and said, "What I need is for you to take me to my mother." I told him what had happened in detail, though I have no idea why I trusted him. Once I finished my story, he told me to be ready when he contacted me.

Around ten days later my phone alerted me that it was time for me to meet with the driver. I didn't tell anyone except my grandfather, who happened to be visiting my aunt's house, my sister Hazar, and my cousin. My cousin was my companion during this period of separation; he was exquisitely good at choosing the right words to set my mind at ease and make me believe that I would be reunited with my family, despite what others were saying.

I said goodbye to them, urging them not to tell anyone that I had left until I had arrived in Lebanon. I had no idea what my fate was going to be, nor whether this driver merited my confidence.

Five hours separated me from the border checkpoint. My heart beat faster with every passing mile, as I tried to convince myself that I had made the right decision and that there was no turning back. At each of the numerous checkpoints that stopped us, my terror increased and my conviction grew that I was going to meet my destiny. I tried to calm down by telling myself that God was with me and that he would never let me be harmed because I hadn't harmed anyone and hadn't done anything wrong.

At one point I ventured to ask the driver whether he had arranged for me to be smuggled in by someone. His answer hit me like a thunderbolt: "Just leave it to God." I emitted a long laugh as I suddenly realized that he hadn't made any arrangements with the authorities but was just planning to leave it to luck. My thoughts raced and images took shape in front of me as I heard my mother's sobs when she found out that they had detained me again.

My heartbeat quickens, my body alternately heats up and cools down. My level of anxiety increases as I recall the place where the ogre resides. I urgently need to go to the bathroom, but my fear and curiosity makes me control myself and attend to my unfolding fate second by second. The soldier peers at me through the car window, but he soon tells us to proceed without asking me a single question. I don't know if I was saved by the Qur'anic verses I recited in the hope that he'd avert his eyes from me, or if the driver, who motioned to him with his head, had given him money. All I remember next are successive pairs of eyes glaring at me, until I hear: "Praise God for your safe arrival."

"I need to go to the bathroom," I tell the driver.

"Where am I supposed to find a toilet now?" he responds.

We find a rest stop on the first stretch of road on the Lebanese side of the border and then, finally, the countdown begins for my reunion with my family.

I'm lost in thought and reverie until I arrive in Nijmeh Square in Sidon where I catch sight of my father crying out: "God is great!" He's in tears as he wraps his arms around me. All the cab drivers there congratulate me, as though they know the whole story. We go with a neighbor to the Sharhabil quarter, where my tearful mother is waiting in the street with a group of women from the neighborhood who are trying to calm her nerves.

* * *

My ordeal didn't end after I'd safely returned to Lebanon—it was transformed into an ever-present nightmare. The dreadful face of the ogre would cause me to wake up sobbing in the night. I lurched between the present and the past, sometimes passing out and losing consciousness without warning. But my parents nursed me back to life, and then I started teaching. I was able to overcome my fears and put my ordeal in perspective when I listened to all the disasters that my colleagues, students, and acquaintances had faced.

Years passed in teaching and I became universally known as "Miss Ruba." My students saw me as their savior, and they always told me that I could do the impossible. Little did they know that I was not even able to fix my legal status on Lebanese soil.

I never stopped wondering what would happen to them and where they would go if I left and disappeared from their lives. Would they wait for me to return?

I conversed with the sea, we traded opinions, and eventually I decided to reveal my decision to it. I said: "We're going to announce a truce, you and me. You'll allow us to reach safety—me, my brother, my son, and my new family—in the summer of 2017. You'll introduce me to a people trafficker whom you've dealt with previously and who was loyal to his charges, delivering people safely across you to the coast opposite Arab lands. I'll reunite there with my real family under one roof and we'll obtain legitimate residency as non-Arabs and we'll renounce the supposed right of return. Yes, I'll endorse my renunciation of you, Palestine, but I'll keep you in my heart, even though you gave me dispersal, oppression, and separation, in addition to my identity."

I adore being Palestinian and having been born in Syria; I adore my Arabness, my land, and my camp, Yarmuk.

I'll ride the sea to you, mother, I'll relish the taste of fear, dread, and turmoil, among the waves of the stormy, raging sea.

I'll come to you, father, in Greece, carrying a diploma in life experience.

I'll meet you, my sister, to assemble a performing arts group composed of the refugees of the diaspora.

I'll come to you, my niece in Germany, to caress you and absorb the scent of yearning and longing from your mother.

I'll come to you, Europe, so that you can issue me a document that states that I'm a human being.

And then I'll return.

I'll return to Lebanon, or Syria, or Palestine.

I'll return to my self.

Or perhaps I won't.

A Migration in Two Exiles

A Diary of the Israeli Invasion of Lebanon 1982

MAHMOUD MOHAMMAD ZEIDAN

(b. 'Ayn al-Hilweh Refugee Camp, Sidon, 1969)

Exodus from the Camp

The camp was blessed with long periods of calm and quiet that could last for hours and days, or sometimes even for months. These were torn to shreds when Israeli warplanes shattered the skies. They would carry out airstrikes, breaking the sound barrier and tracing ominous white contrails on the camp's horizon, or they would bomb a *fida'iyin* military base on the outskirts of the camp, setting off explosions that would take lives and disturb the camp's tranquility. We were used to these upheavals, which resembled the impact of a rock thrown into a still pool of water. The vibrations break the water's surface, which reflects the blueness of the sky, but the rock is ultimately swallowed by the pool, which returns to its former calm and clarity. But the Israeli invasion of 1982, which I lived through, and the accompanying destruction, death, and devastation of the 'Ayn al-Hilweh refugee camp, had a gigantic impact which shattered the surface and clouded the water, an impact which is still being felt at this moment.

One Sunday morning, my mother was boiling the laundry in a metal pot on a fire in front of our house in the camp. The fire was contained by three large rocks, which surrounded some burning tree branches and held up the metal pot whose sides were charred from frequent use. The wood let off gentle popping noises—nothing like the sound of bullets—and the scent of fire conjured up warm thoughts even in the middle of summer. The smell of the laundry soaking in the *nileh*[1] tablets was carried by the steam rising from the boiling water, which mingled with the aroma of the smoke from the burning wood and infiltrated all corners of the house. These sensations arrived at my nose and ears as I sat in the living room studying for end-of-year school exams.

Suddenly, the sounds of an Israeli air raid took over, more powerful than those we'd heard on other occasions. We knew to seek cover in the kitchen, since it was the safest room in the house, being surrounded by other rooms and protected from above by a small attic. Moments later, the sound of a rocket shook the house, exploding shrapnel and strewing debris everywhere. My siblings and their friends scurried down from the roof, falling over each other as they ran for cover. I jumped up from my seat in the living room and ran to the hallway to find out what had happened. It had damaged our house as well as the houses of some of our neighbors. My father went out to the alleyway where my mother was, while my sister escaped to the bedroom.

---

1 Blue tablets that camp dwellers used to place in the water when boiling laundry because it made the colors of the clothes look shinier. They also mixed them with lime when painting houses blue.

Calling out to me and my siblings, my mother ran inside. Since we were little, we'd learned that whenever we heard a rocket's whistle, we were safe, since it meant that it had passed over us.

Dust mixed with smoke filled the neighborhood and a fine white powder settled over the furniture and everything in the hallway. We hadn't heard a whistle, but we were all safe. We thought that it must have fallen in Jabal al-Halib,[2] where there were *fida'iyin* bases often targeted by Israeli planes, or at the bases scattered over Tallit Sayrub.[3] On previous occasions, we would watch the massive planes attacking at low altitude and see them release their rockets, before hearing the terrible sounds of the explosions. Directly after the bombing, we would go and check out the destruction and the huge holes that the rockets made in the ground near the *fida'iyin* bases on the outskirts of the camp. Some of those holes would soon fill with water, making swimming holes for the camp children to play in. I used to think that the holes were so deep that they struck the groundwater, which had poured in to create the pools. I didn't realize that the water came from burst pipes. I never swam in those holes, but I did go with friends from the neighborhood to watch the swimmers. This time, though, for three successive days, we just watched the planes from the rooftops, as they launched their air strikes, and we observed the smoke rising from afar.

Our neighbors' voices could soon be heard:

"That was a close one."

2 The name of a hill scarcely fifty meters high, to the southeast of the camp but outside its perimeter, containing some buildings and *fida'iyin* bases.

3 Another hill, which lies to the east of the camp; many *fida'iyin* bases are located on its barren slopes.

"Go to the shelters."

Everyone rushed to see if there were any casualties. The sounds of the low-flying planes could still be heard hovering over the camp. The rocket had struck my aunt Tamam's house, which was separated from our house by the house of my uncle Muhammad. Part of the ceiling had caved in in the room where Tariq, my aunt's newborn grandson, was sleeping. But he was unhurt because a closet had tipped onto his crib and protected him from the collapsed ceiling.

"There are no injuries."

"Praise God for your safety."

"Let's get out."

"Take the women and small children to the shelters."

The whispers of relatives and neighbors were tinged by terror as we made our way to the shelter of the al-Balad mosque, which was located fifty meters from our house. That shelter had only been built several months previously during a spate of shelter building undertaken by the Palestinian resistance forces. My maternal uncle Qasim and Abu Fu'ad Yunis had taken the initiative to form a committee together with some men from neighboring villages, including Salah al-Khatib from al-Ras al-Ahmar and Abu 'Isam Mi'ari from 'Akbara. They contacted a well-known engineer to help them construct a basement and main hall for a mosque, replacing the old one that was constructed out of corrugated metal. That structure had itself replaced the tent that people from our village, al-Safsaf (in Palestine), used to pray in when they first arrived in 1948. The PLO contributed ten thousand Lebanese liras toward building the new mosque and my uncle offered to collect the rest from emigrants from our village and other camp dwellers. The construction project comprised a mosque and a hall for wedding receptions and funerals, in addition to the basement shelter. Work was completed toward the end of 1981.

We had never entered the shelter before that day. We normally sought refuge in the kitchen, where my mother would embrace us and instruct us, "Say: O kind God, have mercy," and we would repeat the prayer after her. Previous air raids didn't warrant going to the shelters since they never lasted more than ten minutes. The plane would dive down two or three times, each time accompanied by the sounds of anti-aircraft fire. We sometimes went and stood by the mobile anti-aircraft units that defied the planes just to observe the aim of the operator and try to gauge the distance of the exploding rounds. We experienced those moments vividly and didn't hold back our emotions, groaning or clapping, depending on the distance of the anti-aircraft fire from the dive-bombing planes. The gunmen must have found our reactions a source of encouragement since they never tried to dissuade us or chase us away. After the planes had released their rockets into their targets, they would fly off again and we would resume our normal routine.

But that day, nothing seemed normal. The atmosphere was dark and clammy in the shelter, and it smelled like drying clay. The shelter was six meters deep, with a thick roof and heavy walls, and no windows or air vents. A concrete ledge ran along the sides, around forty centimeters high and sixty wide. Some of the camp dwellers spread blankets on the floor and sat in the area in the middle of the hall. The shelter was too small and square to contain our boyish games, which had been shaped by the twists and turns of the camp's alleyways and its random open spaces. We sat among the adults and some of the elderly people, who were annoyed by our constant whispering. In the shelter, all movement was prohibited, as was all talking. Adults would listen to the news, discuss, and analyze. I heard something then that I didn't understand, but I remember well to this day, which was that the aerial attacks were a response to an attempt to assassinate the Israeli ambassador in London, and that Israel was going to invade Lebanon.

We never listened to the news, it wasn't our concern— all we needed was to be released from the grip of the grown-ups. We wanted to make ourselves forget the damp atmosphere of the shelter, the heat of the rockets, and everything going on around us. But they wanted us to just sit there with arms folded, as if we were sitting by a grave or in a classroom.

"No school tomorrow!"

A simple announcement like that could ignite a wave of happiness and bring elation to our hearts. Who doesn't like a vacation? It's the fond wish of teacher and student alike, whether in the depth of winter or the height of summer. Mothers were the only ones who abhorred vacations because they reminded them how tight their houses were and how difficult it was to do their household chores with three or four unruly children sleeping on the floor. But for refugee children, vacations meant we could go wherever we pleased and have whatever we wanted. Vacations opened a space for us in which to release our dreams to take flight in all corners of the universe. When we let our imaginations run wild, we could just cancel out whatever we wanted to, not least the sound of those attacking airplanes.

But the dank shelter restricted our movement and made us feel dead inside. That's why my brother Ahmad and I, accompanied by our cousin Majid and our neighbors Jamal and Hasan, managed to break free of its atmosphere and escape to a room on the ground floor, where we could delight in the open and well-lit space. It was an orderly room, with rows of chairs neatly arranged throughout. We huddled together in one of the corners, across from another, older group of boys, where we could finally play, talk, and better observe what was going on.

But fear began to intrude on our little gathering as the bombing intensified, and we began to ask questions that we didn't have the answers to: "Why are they trying to kill the Israeli ambassador?" Some of us felt glad that militants had tried to kill one of our enemies, even though we didn't understand the word "ambassador." I remember asking: "What does my aunt Tamam's house have to do with an assassination attempt in London?"

Time passed slowly in the large hall where we sat. The sound of each plane would get louder and louder, until it seemed as though it was brushing the tops of the houses, and then came an ear-splitting explosion. The bombing didn't stop. You could hear the bombs in two waves: once deep, as though far away, and then an explosion that rocked our houses and the camp around us. They said that we were being bombarded by naval vessels.

We went back home around noon to have lunch, which my mother prepared while my sisters took turns wringing out the washing and hanging it on the line in the central hallway of our house, since they didn't dare go up to the roof.

The alley in front of our house was crowded with unfamiliar passersby. I rarely saw strangers in the alleys of the camp, which were extensions of the houses and spaces for

neighbors to socialize, cook, wash laundry, meet, and hang
out in the evenings. That day, inexplicable commotion broke
the calm of those alleyways, while the constant sound of
planes, near and far explosions, and the anti-aircraft guns
that defied the planes, filled the air above them. I had no idea
what was going on around me.

Suddenly, the bombing got closer, and the roar of the
planes and the sound of the rockets was deafening. It felt
as though we were in the thick of the battle. The air filled
with dust and smoke, and we no longer heard the whistle of
the rockets.

People were rushing around. My uncle came in and said:
"People are leaving the camp; Israel is now at Ghaziyyeh."[4]

I heard some women whispering: "The Israelis want to
enter the camp."

Others said that the Israelis had arrived at the Awwali
River.[5] Someone else said that they were at al-Kinayat.[6]

My uncle told my father: make sure that each of you has
a knife to defend yourself in case you encounter Israelis.

The people of our village were recalling the memory of
something that they had experienced thirty-four years earlier: when Zionist gangs had attacked the village of al-Safsaf
(in Palestine) and killed nearly seventy men and women and
raped a number of women. After that, the entire population
of the village was displaced. The people of the surrounding villages also fled when they heard about the massacre

---

4 The closest town to Sidon to the south, separated from the camp by a
few orchards.

5 The river located at the northern entrance of Sidon.

6 An area within the camp, at the southern edge, located in the neighborhood of the village of Lubiya (in Palestine).

of al-Safsaf. The decision of the villagers was unanimous: they fled under the devastating impact of the killings. They went to the border village of Rumaysh in southern Lebanon after their villages fell, and the Israelis occupied the entire Galilee region. Then the Lebanese government sent trucks to Rumaysh to carry the people from our village and others to the various camps. From that day onward, my relatives weren't able to return to al-Safsaf.

So my father motioned to my mother, whose memory was imprinted with the events of al-Safsaf, asking her to take me and my sisters and leave with the other people departing the camp. He repeated a well-known saying among Palestinian peasants: "Save the women and children." My grandfather Shihadeh refused to leave his room in the camp despite my uncle Qasim's entreaties. My brother Ahmad had gone to get a falafel sandwich from al-Balawi grocery store. When the bombing intensified, he saw a group of men running hysterically as though they were going into battle. He heard them say that the Israelis were at the entrances of the camp. So he followed them and ended up at the Imam 'Ali mosque, and we had no idea where he went from there.

Every family was trying to find a safe place outside the camp where they could seek refuge. We didn't know where our neighbors or our cousins went. I didn't know where my close friends were, the ones I had just been playing with in the neighborhood and the shelter. I didn't know where we were going. It was usually the father who made decisions to leave the camp, based on his work relationships or other contacts outside. That determined the places people went. The father would convey his decision to other adults, occasionally discussing it with them, but we, the children and the women, never had the right to participate in such fateful decisions. We were like valuable household possessions carried by the family.

My mother was very scared; she had prepared a stew made of gundelia, but we weren't able to enjoy it. She left it behind, gathering us children up and rushing us through the alleyways, chased by the raiding planes, the bombs from the naval vessels, and the bursts of cannon fire from the tanks positioned on the hills overlooking the camp. We left my older brothers behind with the young men who were defending the neighborhood, though they were weaponless and lacked any training.

Cats Don't Eat Spoiled Meat

We took the road opposite the al-Balawi grocery store, passing houses whose sequence I had memorized, and could locate even blindfolded: the house of Abu Fayiz Shraydi, then the house of Abu al-'Abd Farhud, followed by the house of the teacher Fawzi Shraydi, and then the houses of Hani Kraydiyeh, Fatima al-Thaljeh, Abu Nabil Kraydiyeh, Abu al-Shawq, Abu 'Isam Kraydiyeh, and the barber Ahmad Musa al-Taytabani, whose house was on the dividing line between the neighborhood of the people from al-Safsaf and the people from 'Akbara. We went by the 'Akbara spring,[7] and walked up toward the neighborhood of the people from Taytaba, passing by the house of Abu Taha Dahsheh and Abu Nasir al-Khayyat, all the way to the house of the mukhtar, where his widow still lived. Those alleyways are imprinted

---

7 A water source provided by UNRWA in each neighborhood.

in my memory. I made my way through them every evening
in the company of my brother Ahmad, when we used to
sell lupini beans during our summer vacations. We would
call out: "Get some lupini beans!" and would hear a voice
from one of the houses shout: "Over here!" Pinpointing
their location quickly and with precision, we'd head over to
the right door or window to sell our beans. Sometimes a
furtive voice would call out from a window or a rooftop:
"Your grandmother is dancing!" We'd just ignore them and
continue to make our way through the alleys, refusing to be
deterred from our daily mission. We used to make a hand-
some sum that we'd give to our mother for safekeeping, and
she would give it back to us on holidays so that we could buy
new clothes, leaving some to spend as we liked. During the
month of Ramadan, we took the same route through those
alleyways to wake people up for the *suhur* predawn meal.
We'd pass by the windows and call out: "Get up for *suhur*,
Abu Fayiz family! Praise God, Abu Husayn! People, get up
for *suhur*, Ramadan has come to visit!" We'd keep repeating
the chant until someone turned on the light or cried out:
"We're awake!" and then we'd carry on.

Some doors were firmly locked while others were wide
open, signifying to me that the inhabitants were hiding
inside, either because they dreaded leaving or had no place to
go. Or maybe they had left them open like that to welcome
in anyone who might want to seek refuge in their houses.
The roar of planes was growing louder, and the whistle of
rockets was increasingly shrill. I still felt safe in those familiar alleys, though that didn't stop me from being startled by
the sound of rockets every few moments. During our trek,
I looked around me several times to make sure that we were

all still alive and that death hadn't claimed one of us when I wasn't paying attention. I was terrified that one of my family members would be hurt. I felt as though the rockets were following us. On other occasions, we used to be able to see the raiding planes and observe the aim and fire of the mobile anti-aircraft units, as though they were trying to defend us with everything in their power. This time, I felt as though the planes were targeting us specifically, especially since they were flying at very low altitudes and the sound of anti-aircraft guns was beginning to fade, like the faint echo of a groan. Every now and then we'd seek cover against a wall or under an awning, waiting for the planes to fly a little higher. The alleys were crowded with people rushing about frantically, some of whom were carrying simple items suggested by previous experiences of migration, such as mattresses, pillows, blankets, or kitchen pots.

We emerged from the alleyways to the street of the villas, joining hundreds of other people around us. The street was wide and open, lined with low houses whose doorways didn't open right on to the street. I didn't know these houses or their inhabitants and it was at that point that I began to feel fear. I felt like someone who had been stripped of a blanket in the bitter cold. We walked to the Imam 'Ali mosque, where many before us had already arrived to seek shelter. We found my brother Ahmad there. Opposite the mosque was a church where many others had gathered. My father had followed us, carrying some papers and identity cards from the house, which he handed to my mother. He knew to do this from their previous experience when they had to leave al-Safsaf during the Nakba. That time, they had left with nothing.

Before long, there was an altercation among the people sheltering in the mosque. Some of the men from our neighborhood began cursing the young men who had stayed behind to fight in the camp and objected to anyone carrying a gun. My father bristled at their views and countered them vehemently, but he was unable to stop their grumbling and their disaffected stares. At that moment, he decided to leave the place, and as we were making ready to go, we heard that the Israelis had reached Sayrub. My father decided that we should all go to a relative's house nearby, while others decided to go to the public hospital.

We walked behind my father as we passed behind the American school, heading downhill along the only street leading to our relatives' house. The wide street had no houses on it, and no pedestrians were walking there, since it had a clear line of sight to the hills of Miyeh wa Miyeh and Mar Elias. The suffocating silence was broken only by the sounds of the low-flying planes, accompanied occasionally by timid bursts of anti-aircraft fire. We kept to the edge of the street until we found ourselves in front of a two-story white structure. The home of my father's second cousin Yusuf was on the first floor. My father left us there and went to join my older brothers.

The house was calm and still, not like the houses in the camp. When you entered the front door, you found yourself in a living room that was almost ten meters long, with a high ceiling, stylish, plush furniture, and tasteful paintings on the wall. At the eastern end was a window and in the middle was a door leading to the kitchen. Opposite that was another door that led to the bedrooms, and on the western side was a door that opened onto a balcony that looked out

over the playing field of the American school. I really loved
that playing field. Two years earlier, I had played there in the
final soccer match between our neighborhood team and that
of the adjacent neighborhood. The camp's alleyways weren't
wide enough to have proper soccer matches, and the one
playing field on the northeast edge of the camp, near the
public hospital, was a modest dirt pitch, which had that day
been reserved for a match between Abu Ali Iyad's team, the
official team of adults from our village, and the 'Aylabun
team, the official team of 'Ayn al-Hilweh camp. The captain
of our neighborhood team, Rabah, who was five years older
than me, told us that he'd reserved a proper pitch for our
final game, with green grass and stands for spectators. I had
no idea how Rabah managed to secure that pitch. I'd never
seen it before that day or even heard of its existence. I'd never
even set eyes on a green pitch outside of the stadiums whose
pictures I'd seen in the illustrated guides to the 1978 World
Cup. That day, after school had let out, I walked to the pitch
with my brother and the other players, followed by dozens of
kids from our neighborhood who came to cheer us on. We
approached it from the street behind the American school—
at that time, the Imam 'Ali mosque hadn't yet been built—
and entered the field from the rear, clambering in through a
hole in the chain-link fence. I was full of pride and joy that
day as I slipped through the gap in the fence. It didn't occur
to me that this wasn't the main entrance, since I'd never
been in a proper playing field in my life. I was quite taken
by the sight of the green grassy field and the sensation of
my footsteps on it. It felt like the first time I slept on a foam
mattress instead of the woolen ones that we usually slept
on, which never yielded to the weight of our bodies. Less

than five minutes after the match began, I was surprised to see a pack of spectators running out from behind the goal into the center of the field, while others swarmed out of the stands. Kids were shouting and I thought at first that the invaders were trying to disrupt the match because they had been excluded from playing, but then I heard my brother Muhammad calling out to me, and others began shouting: "Run away, quick!"

I ran along with everyone else, not knowing why. The scene of kids scattering resembled an exploding shell fragmenting to fill every available space. We ran as though we were in a race to see who could reach the gap in the fence first. Some climbed over the fence and jumped into the street beyond, while others disappeared behind a row of trees at the end of the field. As I stood waiting for my turn to pass through the hole, I managed to look back at those still hurtling toward me and saw a man running after them, with keys dangling from his waist, carrying a stick in one hand and a pile of clothes in the other. The pitch looked like a battlefield. Some kids were carrying their clothes and shoes, some had stumbled to the ground, others were crying, and the field itself was full of pieces of clothing and stray shoes abandoned or dropped by their owners.

And now I found myself again looking out on that cherished playing field, with no custodian to chase me away.

Yusuf's house was spacious, and his family welcomed us in along with his own siblings, their families, and other relatives: a total of over thirty people. We didn't feel like strangers. Just one pair of green eyes gave us a puzzled looked from the corner of the living room—those of their cat, who wandered around the room checking each one of us out, as if to say: "Where did all these strange faces come from? And why have they come to occupy my house?" Some of us were sitting on the couches and others had made space on the floor, while yet others had found refuge in the kitchen. The cat had no space to roam and its place on the couch had been taken over. There weren't enough seats for all of us and anyone who moved from their seat lost it immediately. The cat startled us whenever it brushed past us. I'm skittish when it comes to cats. I don't hate them—I like them so long as they keep their distance. Our neighbor Nazmiyeh had over ten cats, which she fed and coddled, and most of the cats in the neighborhood congregated at her house. I would see them from afar and never paid them much attention, but now I found myself displaced in the company of a cat, or rather at a cat's house, and so I was obliged to accept the proximity and try not to disturb it.

The bombing resumed and the rockets' whistles got shorter. The building shook but we had no idea where the bombs were falling. We tuned in to the news on the radio, but the radio was not interested in our news or in what was going on around us. We heard the news about distant air raids and battles, in Beaufort Castle (al-Shaqif) and in Khaldeh, on the radio station of the revolution: the Voice of Palestine. That station and the Voice of Arab Lebanon covered events and transmitted coded messages. We heard that the Syrians had entered the battle and that Libya had sent airplanes. That encouraged us and allayed our fears; it made us feel as though we weren't alone in the battle. But then we'd hear a sudden news flash that Israeli planes had downed Syrian aircraft, before the station resumed playing revolutionary songs that we'd memorized and whose rhythms stirred our patriotic sentiments. When I listened to those songs I felt as though we were in a real war that might end with Israel's defeat and our return to Palestine, even though what was happening around us gave no sign of that at all.

On that first night, the women all slept in one room, while the children and some of Yusuf's relatives slept in the living room. The second night, we didn't sleep a wink. The bombing intensified, while loudspeakers from the Imam 'Ali mosque announced that the mosque didn't contain any combatants, so that it wouldn't be bombed by Israel. All the displaced people were asked to leave and some of those seeking refuge in the mosque went to Miyeh wa Miyeh refugee camp, while others headed to the nearby Hamshari hospital, which was still under construction. More of Yusuf's relatives joined us and we all gathered in the living room, women, men, and children, as the bombing reached a terrifying pitch. Each time I felt the space closing in on me, I'd think of the cat and wonder where she went when she disappeared for hours. It became increasingly difficult to stay in that room, since the eastern and western sides were both exposed, and the adults prevented us from approaching the window and the balcony that overlooked the playing field.

I felt a heat inside of me, emanating from the blazing rockets, the roar of the planes, and the June sun, which was more intense than usual. At the same time, the musty air of the shelter filled my nostrils. And the cat was behaving very strangely, curling itself up in a ball, then spreading itself along the floor and extending its tail. This was no shelter!

In the living room, there was a giant ceramic or stone urn, which my older brother had once painted with decorative drawings as a present to Yusuf. The urn was placed near the entrance to the corridor leading to the bedrooms. I liked to admire its green hills, clear blue skies, and flowers. When the shelling intensified, we'd all cluster around it and I could no longer see the hills and sky.

At night, we didn't dare turn the lights on for fear of becoming a target for the planes. But the power soon went out, followed by the water supply, and we started to eat and drink less to avoid going to the toilet. The first day, we ate labneh and cheese sandwiches, and after that, we just ate rice.

The sound of bombing blasted the sleep from our eyes. The cat seemed to feel the air raids coming before we did. I noticed that it would glare at us before we heard the sound of the airstrike, and sometimes would take shelter by the urn before we got there. Cowering there in that small space led me to imagine strange things: I imagined that a rocket would kill us all or that the building would collapse on us. I thought that taking cover beside a closet or door might prevent me from suffocating under the rubble. In that space, all you can think of is death. We held our breath and stopped talking, and my sensitivity to cats disappeared. When the bombing stopped, we'd return to our usual spots, scanning the house to make sure that things were still in place, and we would once again dare to speak or get something to eat. There was some leftover meat in the fridge and our relative Nina decided to cook it with rice for some variety. My sister was worried that the meat had spoiled because of the power cut, so Nina said we should test it. My sister asked: "How?" and Nina said: "If the cat eats it, we can, and if it doesn't then it must be spoiled." So Nina offered a piece of meat to the cat, who ate it, and after that, she and my sister added it to the rice without any qualms.

That meal was a special one; it seemed luxurious after our meatless diet.

We didn't dwell long on our delicious meal, because immediately after lunch a rocket hit the ground floor of the building, injuring one of the neighbors. We were all struck with fright. My mother decided we should go to the Dahduli building nearby, where my uncle, aunt, and their families were staying and which had a basement shelter. We ran in that direction but soon discovered that the shelter was already crowded with people, so we went back to Yusuf's house. Returning felt like going to meet our death, but the bombing had become so intense that we were grateful to have any roof over our heads. An hour later, a rocket hit the Dahduli building. A woman was injured and lost her arm and the daughter of the building's owner was killed on the spot. The bombardment prevented them from taking her to the cemetery, so they buried her in the courtyard of the building.

At around eleven o'clock on the fourth day, another shell fell in the corner of the playing field of the American school. It shattered the glass door of the balcony. So we were forced to seek refuge on the ground floor. A few hours later, another shell hit the eastern side of the ground floor. So we scrambled back upstairs. The bombardment was closing in on us from all sides. We crouched down with our hands on our heads and our heads between our knees, to stifle the sound of the low airstrikes and the noise of the rockets exploding all around us. We had new visions of death. We felt that we could neither stay nor go. The adults decided that we should leave the place, so we gathered ourselves up and went back down to the entrance to the building. We heard a low-flying plane, followed by a softer blast than the sound of the rockets that we'd been hearing. The sky was filled with what looked like shiny droplets sparkling on the horizon, and the adults exclaimed: "Leaflets!" Soon, I managed to see them from where I was standing at the entrance to the building. I hadn't seen aerial leaflets before. We followed them with our eyes as they fell slowly toward us, littering the school playing field. Some also fell near the entrance of the building where we were standing. A few men picked up some of the pieces of paper and started reading: "The Israeli Defense Forces appeal to the people of Sidon not to shelter terrorists. Whoever wants to surrender should carry a white flag and head toward the sea or Miyeh wa Miyeh." Just then, the bombardment subsided and we stood there bewildered, unsure what to do. A few minutes later, the silence was broken by the sound of loudspeakers ordering people to head toward the seashore.

There was no point deliberating any longer. We organized ourselves to evacuate the premises. My older sister held my hand and the hand of my younger sister, and we went out into the street.

The White Sheet

We joined a powerful current of people, individuals and groups from all over, all heading toward the main road leading to the seashore. The sky was clear and blue. The sun was in the middle of the sky, directly overhead, burning our faces and bodies, and it felt as though our brains were being fried. The street was teeming with people, the elderly, women, children, all rushing in a frenzy. Where did all these people come from? Where had they been sheltering all this time? Were there enough houses to take them in? They were looking around periodically to make sure they hadn't left anyone behind. Some of them were carrying clothes, mattresses, blankets, and pillows. Some were holding the hands of their children, as my sister was holding mine, clutching it tightly. I never experienced the Nakba and had never been able to imagine it based on my father's many stories, but I felt that I was living it that day. People were running without knowing where they were going or for how long. No one was talking to anyone else. Some were talking to themselves, or crying, or wailing. My father was stonily silent, and my siblings were too.

The adults had warned us repeatedly: "If you see the Israelis, don't talk to them!"

I walked as though I were in search of something. I'd never seen an Israeli in my life and I was filled with a mixture of curiosity and fear. I wanted to know what he looked like, this person who was trying to kill us, whom we weren't supposed to talk to.

The road from the American school to the convent school was paved with asphalt and it seemed darker than usual. It was covered with dirt and soot, and there were stretches where it had been stripped away by the shelling and others where it had been torn up by the tracks of military tanks. In some places, you could see dark oil stains. It looked as though some small battles had been fought there. Along the sides of the road were many burnt out cars, some of them still smoldering. Electricity poles had been downed and the severed cables crisscrossed our path, making it harder to walk. We saw some dead bodies by the side of the road. I remember one body by the roundabout near the American school and another near a bakery. Some were lying in the large open gutter that ran alongside the Musalli mosque.

We arrived at the post office building, which had been looted and ransacked. The cabinets had been forced open and thrown out of the building. Letters and packages littered the courtyard in front of the building, and some were scattered in the street outside the building and were being trampled. What if some of those letters were ours? Maybe there were letters from friends trying to make sure we were all right, or from my eldest brother, who was studying in Sudan. Some people might be waiting patiently for these letters. Maybe some of them would have changed the destinies of their recipients. Some of them might be old and no longer deliverable based on the addresses. But all of them now lay underfoot, certainly not where they were supposed to be. They had all been stepped on by the feet of those fleeing bombardment and heading toward the sea. We loved that post office and would race to retrieve letters and telegrams to deliver them to their addressees. Anyone who delivered a telegram that specified the arrival date of a loved one, or another piece of joyful news, would get a treat from the addressee. We would avoid delivering telegrams bearing sad news, like the death of someone. Telegrams weren't private and didn't come in envelopes. We would read their few words, which were tersely significant, and then speed off to carry the news to their targets. We competed over who would knock on the door and deliver the news. It was no problem if we startled them; the contents of the telegram would soon bring them joy. They always gave us treats, sometimes to the whole group and sometimes to whoever was carrying the telegram, but we always split the treat among us. The address of the people from our village was: 'Ayn al-Hilweh, Sayrub Intersection, Abu Kamil Yunus shop. All the letters went to that shop. From there, anyone could pick them up from Abu Kamil, who would sort the mail, then deliver the letters or give them to someone he trusted to deliver them. Telegrams got special treatment. They wouldn't wait like letters. They were more expensive, so they usually didn't go to Abu Kamil's shop. Whenever we passed by the post office, we'd check for telegrams and deliver them straight to relatives or our fellow villagers to get our treats. The letters that were being trampled now would never be read and the telegrams that had arrived would never be delivered. There might be people waiting at the airport right now who weren't being greeted by anyone.

People were walking as though in a silent demonstration, with faces contorted by fear and anxiety. I was surprised to see men carrying white sheets draped over their backs and shoulders. They looked different from the people who were carrying mattresses and blankets to use wherever they sought refuge, but I wasn't sure why they were different. After seeing several unfurled white sheets, I asked my sister to explain, and she replied: "It's a symbol of surrender." They were responding to the leaflets that the planes had dumped on us. Then I also began to notice some men carrying women's white veils on the ends of sticks.

We continued walking toward Sidon. The gutter by the side of the road was blocked by cars and dead bodies. As I walked, I was surveying the scene, taking everything in. Sometimes I saw more than what was in front of me. When I saw a body, I tried to imagine what that person had been doing before falling. Then I would notice the tracks made by the tanks and try to guess which way they had gone and wonder whether the *fida'iyin* had confronted them on the side streets. My mind was full of vivid scenes. I felt like I was in a dream or watching a war on a movie screen.

Was this the Sidon I knew? Was this the same street that we walked along one night, joking loudly, breaking the silence of the night and drowning out the buzz of the insects? Why was I feeling such a mixture of fear and sadness?

My relationship to the city of Sidon was not strong, but it was romantic and intimate. We went there during holidays, visiting the holiday carnival and the sea fortress. We walked the alleyways of the old city, buying kanafeh, falafel, wild cucumber pickles, and toys. My eldest brother would take us to the cinema on summer nights to watch kung fu movies and Indian films, then we'd walk back to the camp along this very street, which would echo with our raucous excitement. Sometimes we would visit my uncle 'Awad's house on holidays or when someone was sick. On those occasions we would wear our best clothes, hoping to match Sidon's wide, paved avenues, its tall buildings, and elegant houses.

We crossed the railroad opposite the Arab bakery and found that the tracks had been wrecked. No train would pass there again, and no stories would unfold on those trains. Sometimes we waited by the tracks to watch the trains. I yearned to take the train one day; I had no idea that it was only for cargo. I sometimes saw the conductor riding in the front and he sometimes stopped the train and ran after kids who hung on to the rear cars or tried to clamber onto them. No one from our neighborhood embarked on such risky pranks. We placed nails on the tracks, which would be flattened by the train and become sharpened like knives. We competed over who could walk longer on the tracks without losing their balance and falling. We spent long hours near the tracks, playing on the grass, as though we were in some forlorn and distant forest. There, no one stopped us from running and shouting. Sometimes, we'd go there to study. That was a habit we picked up from older kids, who positioned themselves along the tracks to study for end-of-the-year exams in the spring, in their bright clothes. They looked like colored flowers against the tall green grass.

I suddenly caught sight of the soldiers from the occupation army heading along the train tracks to the north, but I couldn't see them clearly. They were camouflaged and were the same color as the ground. My heart started beating faster and I didn't tell anyone what I saw. We kept walking until we got to the gray Dandashli building, located at the crossroads of Dala'ah and Saraya streets, which was the tallest building in the area. My brother said, "Look at the Israelis on the rooftop!" I looked over and saw that one of the soldiers was looking through large binoculars. As soon as I took my gaze away from the roof of the building, I was surprised to see two Israeli soldiers standing right in front of me like green robots. I was very scared. They didn't look human; they looked like man-shaped objects with metal helmets, black glasses, bulletproof vests, black boots. On their backs, they had what looked like the spray pumps that sanitation workers from UNRWA used to spray pesticides on garbage. But these backpacks had two aerial antennas for their wireless devices. I soon noticed that there were many soldiers behind and around these two, and that we had to pass in front of them to continue. My sister pressed my hand and told me not to look at them. I tried to look away but noticed a soldier extending his hand, as though offering us something. I couldn't see what he was holding and clung more tightly to my sister. He said in broken Arabic: "No be afraid, biscuits." Tugging me toward her and pressing my hand, my older sister replied: "You kill us, then you give us biscuits." I didn't take any, nor did my younger sister, and we continued on our way to the sea.

The procession slowed down as it reached what is now known as Martyrs' Square. The square was packed with people, some standing and others sitting. There were two craters in the square, which had been made either by bombs or by bulldozers. There were many bodies wrapped in plastic bags lying beside the craters. Someone said that they were burying the bodies of those who had been killed in the government hospital. We hadn't heard that there had been a massacre at the hospital. We didn't have time to wonder whether people we knew had died; we were too busy thinking about our journey, whose destination was still unknown.

We passed through the square and continued toward the convent school. I didn't know why we were walking in that direction. We were following my father and he appeared to be following those in front of him.

We walked past the convent school and made our way toward the Dawha school run by the Maqasid association. It felt as though we were in a crowded market with no vendors; each of us was looking for something but no one knew where to find it. A mother was looking for her children, a father was looking for his sons, another mother was looking for a room where she could stash away her little ones, someone else was looking for a loaf of bread for his family. You were met with questions everywhere you looked, and no one had any answers. If you happened to ask someone, you would be answered with another question. Some people asked about my brother who stayed in the camp, others said they saw him there, and yet others claimed to have seen him leaving. Some even said they saw him martyred, and others that they saw the Israelis capture him. My father, mother, siblings, and I entered the schoolyard of the Dawha school and were met by a heap of trash in the middle of it. There were women who were bedded down along the edges of the schoolyard and others who were washing their clothes and their children's clothes in the drinking fountains on another side of the yard. Some people were standing at the classroom windows overlooking the school yard. Clean laundry was hanging from the classroom windows and the noise in that space was louder and more jarring than during recess on a normal school day. I asked my sister why we were there, and she replied that we were looking for a classroom to sleep in.

Soon, we resumed our journey, following my father out of the school. I didn't hear a word from him. Maybe he wasn't talking. I mostly asked my siblings, but sometimes I figured out the answers to my questions by myself: "There are no empty classrooms."

I was overjoyed. It didn't occur to me to ask where we would spend the night. I couldn't conceive that I could sleep in a classroom in that school, or that I would go to the bathroom there, or put up with the deafening noise, or breathe the stale air amid that throng of humanity. It wasn't hard to pick up the same sentiments from the eyes of all my siblings and deduce it from my father's silence.

My father led us through a narrow road opposite the Dawha school, then he took a path behind the houses, and

we ended up in a backyard, where we came across my maternal uncle and his children as well as my maternal aunt's
family. The land belonged to an old, deserted house with
a ground-floor porch overlooking an empty lot with a few
small trees. On the other side of the yard from the house was
a patch of dry grass that had been scorched by the flaming
June sun, and beyond that was a small cemetery. My uncle's
family had already claimed the porch of the house, so we
planted ourselves by a small tree whose shade provided some
relief from the heat of the day. My father left us in that shady
spot and went off somewhere. He was always preoccupied
with my brothers, two of whom were still missing. We didn't
know where they were or anything else about them.

That place was not crowded like the school, only a few
families. There were no men among us, just us children and
women, spread out under the trees. Israeli soldiers were gathering together the older boys and men by the seashore, where
they were forced to sleep at night to make sure that no one
undertook military operations against the occupation. I went
to sit among them on the burning sand. When my brother
and I went back to join my mother and other siblings, the
night sky was clear and the stars were visible through the
leaves of the trees that we were sleeping under. From time to
time, we could hear helicopters, and the searchlight beams
would periodically light up the yard like sunlight then vanish again. Some of our neighbors had hung blankets from
the trees to create partitions between the families that didn't
know each other. That first night we slept calmly, without
the sounds of air raids or bombing.

By the next day, we had eaten all the bread we were able
to carry from our relative Yusuf's house and we went the

whole day without. Everyone was mobilized. One woman promised to give my sister and cousin some bread, so they followed her to the old town of Sidon, traveling through old alleyways that they had never seen before. My sister began to worry that the woman was going to do them harm, but she finally gave them a few loaves, which they took in a hurry. As they made their way back, they couldn't see the bread in the dark alleys, and when they arrived, we realized that the bread was all moldy. We had to throw it away. On the third day, my sisters and cousins prepared some milk-and-rice pudding. We didn't have spoons or bowls, so we took turns eating with the same spoon straight out of the pot. That afternoon, I went with my cousin Majid, who is two years older than me, to buy some bread from town. We met some people carrying loaves of bread, who pointed us in the direction of the old town, which the people of Sidon call "al-Zawarib" (the alleys) or "al-Balad" (the town). We made our way uphill toward the Maqasid school, in the direction of al-Zawarib. Our usual route to the old town, which we took on holidays, went from the 'Akkawi falafel shop at Shakiriya, past the town hall, and down to the seashore, where the carnival was set up for the holiday. This time, we had to approach the old town from the direction of the men's café, past the Maqasid school, and we entered unknown alleyways. We saw plenty of military boots and uniforms abandoned by the wayside, left there by their owners who had fled. Eventually, our lungs were filled with the aroma of freshly baked bread and we came upon a long line of people queued up in front of the Abu Nahleh mosque. There, I saw older boys and men in greater numbers than had been on the seashore, as if all the males of the city had come to buy bread—there were no women there at all. They were all jostling and squabbling in front of the bakery. The owner of the bakery and the workers were refusing to sell anyone more than just one loaf of Arabic bread. We waited more than an hour for our loaf, but we returned empty-handed, raising our arms in surrender.

There was nothing for it but to spend another day without bread. We didn't have a change of clothes, so my cousin and sister went to the house of another cousin, who was in Abu Dhabi, to bring some clothes and flour. His house was near where we were staying. When they got there, they were confronted by the neighbors, who said: "We've been putting up with you (Palestinians) for thirty years, now the Israelis are going to step on your necks." So they came back without entering the house.

We had no bread, no clothes, and no toilets. I don't remember using a toilet during that time, but I saw some of the others going to the nearest part of the cemetery. Groups of girls accompanied one another to answer the call of nature.

The owners of the house arrived and began to curse and insult us. We didn't answer and my uncle's family didn't move away from their spot on the porch, they just made way for them to access the door. We had nowhere else to go. Anyway, they weren't insulting us personally, but Palestinians in general. They went into their house, took some of their personal belongings, and went on their way.

On the fourth day, the Israelis allowed people to go to back to their houses in Sidon, so my sisters and female cousins went to my uncle 'Awad's, whose house we used to visit on holidays, which was close to the Ghassan Hammoud hospital. When they got there, they baked nearly a hundred loaves of bread. The smell of baking bread drew my uncle's neighbor, who was so overwhelmed, he said: "You Palestinians have always been our pride, you're good people." So my sister gave him ten loaves and distributed the rest among our relatives.

All this time, we'd been trying to entertain the little ones to distract them from their hunger, but once the bread arrived, everyone fell silent and was entranced by its magnificence. That afternoon we were able to go buy some necessities from the stores that had been spared from looting and whose owners were able to open them up.

On the fifth day, early in the morning, the occupation army announced over loudspeakers that everyone was to congregate near the entrance to the Dawha school. The soldiers who were speaking had a distinctive accent, which sounded Yemeni or Druze. We saw many military vehicles carrying heavily armed soldiers. After they had gathered all the men in front of the school gate, they began parading them in front of informers hidden in half-track armored vehicles, the likes of which I'd never seen before. The informers had covered their heads with white masks with two holes for the eyes. Even though I was watching from a distance, I was filled with fear. Each man would pass in front of the informer. If he gave a sign, they would pull the man aside, and if he didn't, they would let him go. I remember that the workers from Sri Lanka were all brought up together and the informer pointed at one of them after the other. The soldiers took them all aside. A joke went around that when they were asked where they worked, they answered: "Fateh Company." After that, trucks came to take away all those who had been pulled aside to an unknown destination.

The Israelis branded the identity cards of people who were cleared by making an incision on the side where the picture was and stamping them in Hebrew. New people arrived at the seashore every day and were subject to the same treatment. Everyone was instructed to go to the shore. I went to witness the operation every day. I thought of myself as a young man, which is why I went, but I didn't look old enough, which is why I was never passed in front of the informers. The Israelis ordered everyone over fifteen to go to the shore and they detained many of our friends. One of them was Suhail Abul-Kull, even though he was only fourteen and small of stature. He died later in the Ansar internment camp after one of the protests organized by the prisoners.

On the sixth day, my sisters went back to my uncle's house to check on the extended family and wash some clothes. My uncle told them that he had found an apartment that we could stay in, so we went with my aunt's family as well as my two cousins and their families. One of my cousins had come from Kuwait to spend the summer vacation and had been trapped with us. There were around twenty of us and the new apartment was practically palatial. The living room was ten meters long, with high ceilings, and paintings on the wall. It had three bedrooms and two bathrooms. All we needed was four walls, but God had granted us much more. The men and children spread themselves out in the living room while the women shared the bedrooms.

The Israelis patrolled the city all night. We heard the constant rumble of the armored vehicles and saw the searchlight beams lighting up the balconies. During the day, they announced through the loudspeakers that everyone was to gather in the squares. That night, the men were instructed to come to the large square at Sitt Nafiseh, and line up in the street. The Israelis were going to search all houses for terrorists and kill anyone who stayed behind. People were gripped by fear. Deep inside, I wanted to go down to the square near our new apartment, to prove that I was no longer a child, and to join my friends and neighbors who had been captured and taken to the Ansar internment camp. But my sisters were unpersuaded and stubbornly prevented me from going, saying: "You're not fifteen yet!"

They even stopped my sixteen-year-old brother from going, while my eldest brother just refused on his own.

Every morning, we would find Energa anti-tank rifles or Kalashnikov (AK-47) rounds piled up in front of the entrances to some of the buildings. People were dumping them furtively at night. Holding or possessing a weapon was a serious charge, and some people began to tell the Israelis about the presence of weapons in their buildings.

I was surprised by the number of weapons caches and offices of the Palestinian resistance in Sidon. Some of the offices had distributed relief supplies, while others served other purposes. The underground shelter of the building that we were living in had a depot filled with blankets, military uniforms, and a few small arms. Almost every building in our neighborhood had some sign of the resistance, as we came to realize watching Israeli military trucks park outside each one to seize their contents. The depots were full of new and unused supplies, and confiscating all the property took many hours. It was a sad and shameful sight.

The Israelis soon propagated the use of the term "terrorist" (*mukharrib*) to describe the Palestinian resistance fighters (*fida'iyin*). They commanded civilians not to shelter terrorists, and then raided their houses, forcing doors open with their boots, brandishing their rifles, and illuminating their surroundings with glaring lights.

They would ask: "Are there any terrorists here?" The term became so widespread, that some Lebanese started using it to describe Palestinians. Even Palestinians would reply to the Israelis saying: "There are no terrorists here," rather than calling them *fida'iyin* or fighters.

Early one morning, as we were asleep in the living room, there was a loud knock on the door to our new apartment. My aunt opened the door and engaged in a dialogue. The voices echoed in the empty apartment building, but we couldn't understand what was going on. She returned and said: "Israelis." Then she went to the bedrooms and woke up the women and girls, saying: "Don't be afraid, the Israelis want to search the house, don't panic."

My sister threw some bedclothes over my eldest brother, who had not gone to get his identity card stamped, and sat on top of him on the bed. Moments later, five heavily armed soldiers entered, accompanied by the neighbor to whom we had given some bread. When they got to the bedroom where my brother was, my sister called out: "We're all women and children here."

The soldier retreated. They proceeded to search the rest of the house, entering each of the other rooms in turn. One of them turned to our neighbor and said: "Who says there's a terrorist here? There are no terrorists."

The soldiers apologized and offered candy to the children, but we refused to take it.

Between Two Exiles

The camp still held some fighters who refused to surrender
and leave. Israel sent some of the elders to negotiate with
them at al-Kifah school to get them to surrender. But the
fighters responded by saying: victory or martyrdom.

After eleven days of intense bombardment, 'Ayn
al-Hilweh camp fell. The number eleven has a special meaning that many Palestinian refugees might not be aware of, even
those who live in the camp and its surroundings, let alone
those who live outside that circle. But some of us refugees,
along with the Israeli occupation army, are highly attuned to
that number and will never forget it. It's common knowledge
among those who follow such things that the Israeli occupation army arrived at Bhamdun (in the Shuf mountains of
Lebanon) while 'Ayn al-Hilweh was still resisting, and it's common knowledge among those who follow such things that the
Israelis ran into trouble in the camp for eleven days straight.
Those who put up the fight and gave them such trouble were
eleven men, ranging in age from sixteen to forty-three. We
found this out from one of the fighters, who confided in us
the whole story, saying: "There were just eleven of us." The
Israelis never found out the number of fighters. They were
eleven planets orbiting not the sun, but fire and gunpowder.
They would come up from behind the Safsaf mosque to face
the maelstrom of fire. A giant Merkava tank unleashed its
barrage on the houses of the camp, reducing them to scattered rubble. The men attacked it from behind, destroying it
and preventing other armored vehicles from advancing. By
engaging with the enemy at close range, they also prevented
the air force from being effective for eleven days.

The day the men withdrew, the fighting stopped and the inhabitants of the camp were permitted to inspect their homes. The directive from the occupation army said: enter at 7:00 a.m. and leave before 9:00 a.m., at which point bombardment will resume. Anyone remaining in the camp would be considered a "terrorist."

We followed my father to the camp, along with thousands of others. Most people entered in a hurry and left in even more of a hurry, carrying mattresses and household items salvaged from the ruins of their homes. I found myself torn between my fearful impulse to leave and my longing to stay cradled in my birthplace. Fear and longing. I'd never been away from the camp for such a long time. I yearned for our little neighborhood and the alley that we played in, for our house and the grapevine that we sat under, to study or just to relax. I wanted my things, the toys and storybooks my eldest brother had bought for us. But the anxiety and fear that the bombing could resume at any time crowded out my yearning.

We walked along the main street, which was broader than it had been, now that the houses and shops that once lined it had been razed to the ground. The wreckage piled at either end of the street now served as a barrier that protected the tanks and armored vehicles of the occupation army. We arrived at a vast open square, the likes of which had never existed before in our camp. We were dumbfounded as we compared the scene to the topography of the site that was stored in our memories. That was where you took the road to Sayrub, an intersection we knew well, which led to our neighborhood. A fierce battle had clearly taken place there. A burnt-out Merkava tank was still smoldering and there were signs that soldiers had been killed there. Later, I learned that it had been the most ferocious battle of the war and one in which the young men had taught the occupation army a lesson. It was the Sayrub intersection after all, but there was hardly any sign left of the people who had lived there, or the stores that had marked the spot. I could make out the ruins of the Safsaf mosque, which had collapsed onto the underground shelter where people had gathered, and where people used to congregate on somber occasions to pay condolences. The elderly people and those who were with them, who had sought refuge in the mosque's underground shelter, had all perished. From that time onward, it was renamed the Martyrs' mosque. And there, too, I saw what remained of Abu Hamad's coffee shop, which used to sell thick Arabic coffee whose aroma roused the nose of every passerby and stirred all nearby sleepers. It was the site where people had spun so many stories of youthful heroics and told memories of a lost homeland. Abu Marwan was a *hakawati* (storyteller) who never tired of relating accounts of his exploits in the final battle for Safsaf during the Nakba, or telling exotic tales that would keep the customers riveted and the coffee flowing. Coffee cups had been shattered and companions scattered, and the dark brown liquid that had been held delicately in the cups had no place among the ruins.

Next door were the remnants of Muhammad Dib's shop, where we bought falafel and ful, and ice cream in the summer. And next to that, the ruins of Abu Kamil Yunus' shop, our mailing address. Abu Kamil was a gentle soul, with a slow robotic walk, who gave us sugar-coated almonds while we played. We couldn't figure out why he walked like that. Some said the Israelis had shot him, but we weren't able to find out how or why. We finally gathered that he was the only survivor of the dreadful Safsaf massacre. At the time, Abu Kamil was on his way back from the flour mill in Bint Jubayl in southern Lebanon, not realizing that Safsaf had fallen to Zionist militias and that the fighters in the village had been forced to retreat. When he arrived at his house, he was startled by two Israeli soldiers, who grabbed his arms and held him back. He had been distracted by the sight of his son, Kamil, running toward him to get the candy that he always brought back from his trips to the flour mill. As the Israeli soldier restrained him, he managed to throw the candy, saying: "Take this, son, the last gift from your father."

He had no idea that he'd survive that day. The Zionist militiamen took around fifty young men from the village, who had been hiding in the houses of the village elder and Isma'il al-Nasir, lined them up against the wall, and sprayed them with bullets. Abu Kamil was injured and fell to the ground, while another man holding a child fell onto him. He had only been lightly wounded in the arm. Later, he attempted to get up and join the women, but he glimpsed the soldiers returning and lay back down, pretending to be dead. He had learned Hebrew from having worked in Haifa, and he heard the soldiers say: "Finish off anyone who's still alive."

He held his breath and froze. More bullets penetrated his shoulder and thigh. That's how he survived the massacre of Safsaf in 1948, though he continued to walk with a limp because of the injuries he had sustained. And he always distributed candy to the children, just as he had done with his son, Kamil. Had the Israelis now finally tracked him down and killed him? Had they really destroyed his shop, the candy warehouse for us kids? There, for sure, was where the shop had been. And that's where our mail went. The Israelis had sent us a clear message: you won't get your mail here anymore. We were now without an address. This was where I was from, but it was no longer what it was, and I was over there now, in Sidon, where I had no roots or memories.

There was no sign of our neighborhood apart from the mosque, which we could make out because of the wreckage of the main hall and the remains of the minaret. The landmarks had all been wiped out and we lost all sense of direction. We climbed over the ruins of the house behind the mosque and headed eastward across a wide expanse of rubble to get to my aunt's house. From there, perched on the debris, we could see the dark blue sea. We could never see it before because of the houses, trees, and grapevines. Now, it sparkled clearly in front of us, appearing very close. We made our way through the neighborhood until we arrived at our house, which still stood, even though the walls were pockmarked and full of holes from the rockets. The surrounding houses were partially destroyed and coated with a fine layer of white dust, like flour.

The neighborhood was still there but it was demolished. The alley near our house where we used to play was blocked by rubble and fragments from nearby houses. Our neighbor Abu Salih would scold us every time we played football there. The doors of his house were blown out and we didn't know if he was dead or alive. He would never scold us again because no one would be able to disturb his peace ever again. The neighborhood seemed ghostly, stripped of the sounds of children playing and mothers yelling, of kerosene stoves and revolutionary music from the 1970s. "My weapon springs from my wounds." All those sounds had fallen silent, but they still echoed in my head. Now and then, as I trod on the rubble, I froze when I heard what sounded like a death rattle that echoed in the neighborhood and drowned out the other sounds reverberating in my head. Suddenly, I heard a loud crash and stopped in my tracks in terror, thinking that the Israelis were attacking us. It was just one of our neighbor Nazmiyeh's cats! It had stepped on some debris, sending a rock clattering down on to a piece of tin metal roofing. The cats were wandering around the neighborhood, apparently looking for Nazmiyeh. Meanwhile, my father was absorbed inside the living room of our house, hurriedly sorting through the books, putting some of them in large flour sacks so that we could take them with us, and hiding those about the Palestinian cause to prevent the Israelis from discovering them. He had lit the stove and was burning some papers and other effects that I knew nothing about.

As my sister and I inspected the rubble of houses, we found a Simonov rifle abandoned in the wreckage. We carried it to our house. My father told me and my sister to bring some old clothes, then he proceeded with great speed to lock the house door and dig a hole in the flower planter. He said that we were going to bury the rifle right there. My sister and I wrapped the rifle with the rags and plastic and buried it. Then we replanted the flowers and other plants on top of it. We did all that with record speed, as though it was something that we did all the time. But only my father knew what he was doing and why. I felt his reluctance to discard the weapon and saw the apprehension in his eyes for what the future would bring. He had understood the value of weapons ever since he and his four cousins had pitched in to buy a rifle in his village of Safsaf, to protect themselves against the same occupier.

We wiped our hands and my father went back to filling the bags of books, which we carried out, making sure to leave before 9:00 a.m. Other people were carrying all sorts of necessities rescued from their houses that they needed for their daily lives. Me, my brother, sister, father, and mother were all carrying books from my brother's extensive library. People were giving us strange looks. Maybe they were bemused by the sight of us sneaking books out of our house. One of our relatives said: "Take something that might be useful!"

We kept up our book rescue operations for three consecutive days. On the second day, I was accompanied by my cousin Majid. We wandered alone while my father was sorting the books and other things. Majid was carrying a camera at the time, so I said: "Let's take pictures of ourselves."

I took a picture of him standing on the ruins of his house, then he took a picture of me on the same spot. Their house was really three houses in one: there was my uncle 'Awad's old house, and my aunt's original house, as well as a house that my cousin Muhammad, who worked in Saudi Arabia, had built twenty years ago but never lived in. We managed to clamber to the top of the heap of rubble. The view wasn't panoramic or beautiful in any way. All we could see were the ruins of smaller houses. They had all been levelled to the ground, all the way to the dark blue sea. But we could already glimpse the sea from below, without needing to scale the rubble, since the horizon was totally open. There was an eerie silence in the neighborhood, but as we walked on toward our house to help my father sort the books, the sounds of a hubbub gradually reached our ears. At first, we thought it was Nazmiyeh's cats again, but the sound kept getting nearer and louder and soon, we were startled to see a group of occupation soldiers standing in the doorway of our house. They shouted at my father: "Hey, you!" "Yes," my father replied from inside. "What you doing?" added the soldier in broken Arabic. My father responded in a similar idiom, "Me clean house." The soldiers entered the house with the barrels of their guns pointed at my father and motioned to him to show them the bedrooms. He went first and they followed him. Then they led him outside, and we thought they were going to arrest him, so we walked behind them. They took him to our neighbor Abu Salih's house and told him to go down to the basement shelter. He took the steps down and they followed. After that, they just said: "Enough, go home!" My father returned and asked us to help him carry the books and leave.

On the third day, one of our relatives asked me and my brother Ahmad to go to one of the underground shelters in the Samiriyeh neighborhood to fetch a pair of night vision binoculars that he and some fighters had taken from one of the tanks that they had disabled. Before the invasion, I knew Samiriyeh's alleys by heart. We passed through the neighborhood on our way to the lower mosque to perform the five daily prayers. For the dawn prayers, my eldest brother would wake us up and walk with us. We'd hang on to him as we passed the Khraybi house, where there was a swing and a big dog. When the dog heard our footsteps, he would start barking and keep at it until after we'd passed. My brother would tell us not to be afraid and not to run. He'd say that if the dog knows you're scared, he'll run after you and bite you if he manages to catch you. We couldn't contain our fear, but we trusted our elder brother and followed his advice. We maintained an outward calm, while inside we were anything but. Every time we walked past, my knees rattled like an electric sewing machine and my teeth chattered loudly. But as my brother promised, the dog would tire of barking as we walked by without looking at him or picking up the pace, and he would then retreat, allowing us to continue on our way.

We went to that place now, as our relative had instructed us, without fearing the dog, but we couldn't find any trace of the shelter. We searched in that wide expanse of rubble but found ourselves going around in circles. We'd walk back toward the houses that were still standing to find our bearings, then retrace our steps. We hiked along a path by the ravine that we used to take to the lower mosque. The ravine was full of discarded weapons. We slipped down to a shelter in the ravine, but it was empty save for some discarded Kalashnikov rifles and empty jars of honey that appeared to have been consumed by the fighters. We walked back over the ruins of levelled houses to look for another shelter. Where could that place be? We couldn't even find the house with the swing and the dog. Other people passed by us as my brother and I kept going around in circles. After some time, we found an opening in the ground leading to a shelter, which had been covered by a flat piece of metal. There were broken doors and pieces of rubble blocking the entrance. Ahmad and I looked around to see if anyone could see us, but the passersby were looking straight ahead. With my brother leading the way, we decided to go down into that shelter. We lifted the metal cover to find a very dimly lit space, the only light filtering in from the opening. We crept into the underground shelter, treading carefully, not knowing what we were stepping on. Slowly we began to make out some shadows. We saw rocket-propelled grenades and Kalashnikovs leaning against the walls, cans of food, and other supplies. Finally, we found a small pair of binoculars. We didn't think it matched the description, but we took it anyway and left in a hurry, without bothering to investigate or search the place any further. We just wanted to complete the mission and demonstrate that we had been there. My brother hid the binoculars in his clothes and we climbed out of the shelter. We ran all the way to our house in the camp and concealed them in one of the book bags, and then returned to the place we were staying at in Sidon. The next day, we gave the binoculars to our relative, who confirmed that they were not the right ones.

The Israeli occupation army was preoccupied with the battle for Beirut and was worn out by the fighting. Meanwhile, life began to return to Sidon gradually and things started to seem normal. We felt that it was time for us to return to the camp, but we weren't allowed to, so we became residents of Sidon. Our apartment there was nice and large, but crowded, and we rarely emerged from it. Israeli forces regularly patrolled with loudspeakers calling on people to gather in the street or announcing a curfew. We only ventured outside to visit the camp, bring necessities, or fetch books. I experienced a harsh exile in Sidon. I had no friends there and I didn't know the neighbors. Their doors were always shut and we never greeted each other on the stairs. I felt like a stranger in the same Sidon streets that I had loved as a child. Our trips to the camp grew more frequent and we started hearing reports that UNRWA was distributing building materials to people so they could rebuild their houses there.

Some people began to go back to the camp, especially those who were staying in schools, orchards, and garages. We decided to return, too, but this decision wasn't like our decision to leave, because it wasn't unanimous. My eldest sisters, my mother, and my middle brother decided to stay in the apartment with our relatives, while my father, elder brother, other sister, and I wanted to go back to the camp. The camp was like a wasteland. Most of the youths and men were at Ansar internment camp. As for my brother and I, we were no longer children. We saw ourselves as men, although our mustaches hadn't sprouted yet. During those first days, we slept on the roof of our house with my paternal uncle's family, my maternal aunt's family, and the neighborhood kids—an assortment of men, women, boys, and girls. We all spread out in the open air, counting the stars. We burned cow dung to fend off the mosquitoes and other bugs. The insects proliferated because of the wreckage and garbage, the burst water pipes and damaged sewers, and maybe because there were human and animal bodies buried under the rubble. In the early days, informants roamed through the camp wearing masks and raiding houses during the daytime. Later, they began to move around without masks, but they didn't dare enter the camp's alleyways alone at night.

One day a group of kids was playing in a burnt-out jeep that had belonged to the *fida'iyin*. It was in a nearby orchard that was once called the Jewish orchard, and later renamed the Jerusalem orchard. They were playing across from a jeep full of Israeli soldiers. One of the soldiers began to ridicule the kids, so one of the kids picked up a rock and threw it at him, hitting him in the head and drawing blood. The kids scattered in all directions, but the soldiers were incensed. They gave chase and began to shoot in all directions. Then they encircled the vicinity and launched a search for the boy who had thrown the rock. The neighborhood emptied of children as the soldiers began breaking into houses. They found Ayham, son of the teacher 'Ata Du'aybis, eating lunch with his mother in their house, and tried to arrest him. But his mother kept crying and imploring them not to take him until they left him alone. We dared not stir from the attic where we were hiding until nightfall.

We spent our days clearing out the rubble from the neighborhood, and at night we stayed up and kept company with the adults. Every two or three days we went to Sidon to check on the rest of the family and friends, as well as to get food and bathe.

When word came to us that the municipality of Sidon was hiring people to paint the city walls, paying five Lebanese liras per day, I was eager to sign up. My school had been destroyed and I needed a way to fill my time. So I got myself hired along with some of the neighborhood kids and began painting the walls that bordered the main streets of Sidon. When I collected my first week's wages, I bought a grown-up bike. It was a Hercules-brand bike and I was smitten with it. I also bought new clothes for the 'Id holiday with the money I earned from that job. But the whole thing ended badly for me. One day, we were painting the walls of an orchard alongside the road that joins the Sitt Nafisa and Sabbagh neighborhoods, near the olive oil press. A BMW car pulled up nearby and the driver, a man in his late twenties, called out loudly to us. We began walking toward him, thinking that he had lost his way and needed directions. But when we approached, he pointed an M-16 rifle at us and shouted: "Get in the car! Quick!" "Why? What have we done?" we answered nervously. "Get in, you dogs, fast!" he replied.

We began to panic, but just at that moment another car approached from behind and the man sped away. We fled in the opposite direction, not pausing for breath until we reached the house of the municipal engineer Jad Sha'ban, who was supervising our work. He reassured us and told us that he would inform the mayor's office. But we jumped on our bikes and raced back to the camp, never to return to that job.

That day marked a souring in my relationship to the city of Sidon. I spent most of my days thereafter in the camp.

Two Masks and a Darkness

The camp became a haven and a place of solace. There, we could meet and feel secure despite the fear provoked in us by the informants, despite the exodus of the Palestinian resistance movement and the absence of the men being held in the Ansar internment camp, and despite the omnipresent darkness. There was still no electricity in the camp, so we relied on candles and kerosene lamps. Neighbors would gather at night, often at our house, to reminisce about the days before the war, and to exchange analyses of the current political situation and what might become of the refugees. The comfort of staying up late sharing stories helped us to overcome the darkness and our trepidations about the future. Each time one of our relatives or neighbors returned to live in the camp, we rejoiced in their arrival, and our ties of affection and solidarity were strengthened. The camp became a magnet for displaced people. One day we were wandering through the alleyways and caught a glimpse of a cousin who had been in Bulgaria on a training course. Someone said: "That's 'Adnan!" We couldn't believe it. Why would 'Adnan come back from Bulgaria at this time? We had seen him slip by like a ghost, moving very quickly. So we sped off to the house of my uncle, his father, and scanned the ruins, but there was no sign of anyone. 'Adnan had managed to slink away so stealthily that it made us doubt our own senses. Later, we realized that many young men had returned from abroad to mobilize and fight, only to find that the war was over by the time they arrived. The *fida'iyin* had already departed for new, unfamiliar exiles.

I can still picture the scene of the resistance fighters departing from Beirut in 1982. It was the end of an era and the beginning of the unknown. Thousands of fighters were transported in trucks belonging to the Lebanese army, waving Palestinian and Lebanese flags. It was a poignant moment. Women were tearing up, as were men. On television, we watched as Lebanese politician Walid Junblatt fired a gun in the air to lament the exit of the fighters. Bursts of gunfire erupted here and there, in mourning or in celebration, while the fighters flashed victory signs. In our home, as in our neighbors' homes, a deep sadness enveloped us all. The men knitted their brows. We couldn't comprehend what had happened. Just days earlier, we were following reports of fierce battles in Beirut and its surroundings, monitoring the radio broadcasts daily. The battles in the southern suburb of Khaldeh, at the Beirut airport, at the Lebanese Museum. We'd heard that the occupying army hadn't managed to advance past the front lines in Beirut, and we'd watched as Israeli convoys of supplies and reinforcements traveled northward past Sidon toward Beirut, warplanes roaring overhead as they ran support missions and carried soldiers to and from the city. But now, that was all over. The *fida'iyin* had left. Abu 'Ammar (Yasir 'Arafat) had left. I used to dream that when I grew up, I would join the revolution. We had been steeped in the conviction that the *fida'iyin* would liberate Palestine. But now I watched as they left us, just when we needed them most to protect us. Palestine receded from my consciousness at that moment. All I could think about thereafter were the terrifying nights in the camp, the informants, the Phalangist forces, and the militia of Sa'd Haddad.

I'll never forget the front cover of the Lebanese newsmagazine *al-Hawadith* the week that the fighters withdrew from Beirut. It showed young men carrying their weapons aboard military trucks, stranded in a throng of thousands of mothers, sisters, relatives, and friends who were seeing them off. It was a strange picture. And it generated in me intense emotions of sadness and fear. I hadn't witnessed the fighters battling over 'Ayn al-Hilweh camp, and the thought of that didn't particularly sadden me, but I was devastated by the sight of their departure from Beirut. Later, I painted the scene in oil. That event completed a tragic picture that had taken shape in my mind. The real *fida'iyin* were either martyred or imprisoned, and the last remaining fighters were exiting the country and leaving us behind. I had no use for the traditional leaders who fled, or those who later became collaborators with the occupation army.

Israel succeeded in destroying Beirut, while 'Arafat assumed a position of epic steadfastness, which ended in mid-August 1982 as a result of the negotiations that arranged for Italian and French ships to evacuate the Palestinian fighters to Tunisia, Algeria, Yemen, and Sudan. My pride triumphed over my sense of dread when I heard that Italian ships were involved. Like most people in the camp, I had been following the World Cup soccer tournament that summer, and when the Italian team won the cup, they'd dedicated their victory to the Palestine Liberation Organization to express their support for the steadfastness of the Palestinian people and their resistance to the Israeli offensive. From then onward, my love for the Italian football team grew by leaps and bounds.

Life in 'Ayn al-Hilweh camp had begun to lean toward the "normal." People were restoring the houses that could be saved. Later on, we learned that when the occupation army was unable to storm the camp and gain complete control, it had begun to raze houses to the ground with a huge military bulldozer, on the assumption that removing the houses would prevent fighters from hiding in them and mounting ambushes. Those who could afford to do so refurbished their houses without waiting for assistance from UNRWA or the international organizations and NGOs that proliferated in the camp. Some modest economic activities began to return, and my family set up a small stand selling candy and household items.

But our hope was crushed when we heard that, in the absence of resistance, the occupying army had infiltrated Beirut and occupied the city. They rounded up anyone who was deemed to be related to the resistance in any way, Lebanese or Palestinian. Then we heard about the massacre of refugees at Sabra and Shatila. That struck fear in our hearts. We worried that we would be next. Urgently, we felt the need to have the fighters at our side.

We began hearing about the growing presence of Phalangist militias in Sidon and to the east of the city. We also received reports of incursions by Sa'd Haddad's militia, who abducted people from their homes or detained them at random checkpoints. Once, we heard that the Phalangists were going to attack our camp, so the people living in the houses along the main street, near the camp's entrance, took refuge in our neighborhood and stayed in our houses. We didn't dare shut our eyes that whole night, or for several nights after. Anxiety generated endless discussions that dragged on until the first rays of dawn. We couldn't keep quiet, since silence only heightened the fear.

Our neighbors slept alongside us on the roof of our house for a long time. Our bedrooms and living room were on the ground floor, but we avoided sleeping there so as not to be easy prey for attackers. The living room had three windows, one looking out on the courtyard, another on our neighbor Abu Salih's backyard, and the third on the backyard of my aunt's house. These windows ordinarily stayed open, but we began closing them at all times.

My sister and I were terrified of being massacred. I wasn't afraid of bombardment, which led to a sudden and painless death, but death by massacre took time. That was a whole different, painful matter. It brought up memories of the slaughter of sheep or chickens on feast days and other occasions. The slaughtered animals wriggled and twisted, and the blood spattered all over. The thought made my hair stand on end. We slept with knives under our pillows and the distances between us melted away.

Fear was our daily obsession. It marked the beginning and end of every day. We feared being massacred, and we feared the informants who raided houses at night accompanied by Israeli patrols. They did this whenever they caught wind of the presence of a young man, aged eighteen or older, in the camp. Whenever we heard the rumble of Israeli military vehicles approaching at night, we rushed to hide in one of the rooms. We locked the doors and blew out the candles. Before, we used to go to the rooftop to watch airplanes bombing from the sky, but now we just stayed hidden in the dark, holding our breath.

Fear narrowed the scope of our lives. The growing presence of informants and spies made our lives even more constricted and controlled. Some camp residents began to appeal to the informants to ask for the release of their sons, or to inquire about them in the Ansar detention camp. Their assistance was also sought in securing building supplies or travel permits. That's how they came to have influence over our daily lives and in providing basic services. The occupation army chose thugs, addicts, and people with bad reputations to be their eyes and ears. But many people refused to deal with the informants, rejected their growing role, and despised them.

Some began to organize to confront the informants. They wore masks and moved around at night, transporting weapons and hiding them. We didn't know their names but suspected that some of them were our friends and neighbors, particularly those who weren't present at our evening gatherings or didn't sleep alongside us. One day, the masked men beat up someone from the neighborhood whom they suspected of collaborating with the informants. We feared the sight of the masks. We were used to the *fida'iyin*, whose faces we saw, but not to people in masks that covered their faces. The first time I had seen someone with a mask on had been that day at the seashore when the masked collaborators were picking out the *fida'iyin* from inside Israeli military vehicles. This phenomenon puzzled me: it was as though the informants had now taken off their masks and given them to the resistance fighters. The unmasked informants controlled our lives during the daytime and the masked men controlled them at night, and we feared both.

We slept on the rooftops, men and women, children and young adults. There was nothing separating us from the starlit sky—unless the Israelis overpowered the faint light from the stars with their search beams. That happened whenever those in masks fired on the informants, and sometimes for no reason.

Some of the masked men were fighters who had managed to sneak back into the camp covertly. They gradually gained influence in the camp, appearing in other neighborhoods, and then they began killing ordinary people, without adequate reason. People began speculating and arguing as to whether their victims were collaborators with Israel. Some were keen to indict the victims, as though these unknown, masked individuals were impartial judges passing just verdicts. The masked men began to move around in the camp's alleyways in broad daylight, which made the atmosphere more tense, since there was a greater chance of running into them as we went about our daily lives. They could just kill us and get away with it, since their identities were unknown. Once, my uncle Qasim approached one of them and said: "I'm an old man and even I'm afraid of you. If the children see you, they might pee their pants!" My uncle urged the masked man not to circulate during the day, but he just patted my uncle on the shoulder, saying: "Move along, *hajj*."

The masked men started to harass the neighborhood kids. They would hit one of them for no reason, or scare one because he said something that wasn't to their liking, or take one in for interrogation in the middle of the night and then release him. It was hard to know who was with us and who against us. The camp now harbored factions with leaders and members. Some of those who had left Beirut with the resistance were paying young people to join them. We could hear clashes at night, but we couldn't tell who was fighting who. It was chaos and I felt as though I was always in the dark. We went back to sleeping on the lower level, but always made sure to lock the doors tight.

In fall, it was time for us to return to school. UNRWA set up tents to serve as classrooms but some of them were burned down by the camp's inhabitants, including some students, as a way of signaling their refusal to return to the early days of being refugees and staying in tents that were blown away by storms. We weren't too sad about that because we weren't in a hurry to go back to school. The truth is that we had forgotten that we were students.

My parents enrolled me in a private school in Sidon, and so I bid farewell to the camp. But the Sidon that I once loved had changed. The Israelis had altered its landmarks. They had bulldozed the orchards that once sheltered *fida'iyin* and had served as launchpads for some of their heroic operations. They had dug wide roads and imposed curfews. There was no longer any space or time to play in the city. And we had been too anxious to walk the streets ever since the kidnap attempt by the man in the BMW. At home, we no longer gathered at mealtimes, as we always had growing up. Now some of my siblings were in Sidon, while others had returned to the camp, and still others had moved to Beirut. The family had been destabilized and remains so to this day.

Sidon transformed us gradually, but the upheaval of the invasion disturbed our lives abruptly and profoundly. The place that had united us was devastated, and many families had been dispersed. The camp was full of outsiders. Before, each neighborhood had brought together people from the same village and their relatives. Our doors were always wide open and the gates to houses were unlocked. All that had changed.

At the time, we had no idea of the extent of the fragmentation in the camp. We only knew that the invasion had stolen our childhood; it killed our desire to play. We no longer felt like children.

Life in the camp was no longer calm and tranquil like a pool of water reflecting the blueness of the sky. The ripples that broke its surface now led to powerful currents. I felt dizzy, like a lurching wrestler who was about to keel over. When wrestlers fall, they hit the floor, but I felt as though there was no ground under my feet. I left the camp that I adored to live in a city that seemed unfamiliar to me.

Everything changed from that day onward. Everything.

Glossary

'abaya: traditional robe-like garment worn in many parts of the Arab world

'Abdul Wahab (Muhammad 'Abdul Wahab): renowned Egyptian composer, performer, and singer (1900–1991), who composed songs for Umm Kulthum and other artists

Abu 'Ammar (Yasir 'Arafat): longtime head of the PLO from 1969 to his death in 2004

Abu Hasan Salameh ('Ali Hasan Salameh): senior PLO official who was assassinated by Israel in Beirut in 1979

Abu Jihad (Khalil al-Wazir): senior PLO official who was assassinated by Israel in Tunis in 1988

Abu Mazin (Mahmud 'Abbas): senior PLO official who was elected president of the Palestinian Authority in 2005

'Ain al-Rummaneh bus: a bus carrying armed Palestinian fighters through the Beirut suburb of 'Ain al-Rummaneh on April 13, 1975, which was attacked by Phalangist militiamen, an event that served as the spark that ignited the Lebanese civil war

al-'Asifa: armed wing of the Palestinian political party Fateh

Ansar: an internment camp set up by Israel during its 1982 invasion of Lebanon near the village of Ansar in southern Lebanon to hold captured combatants and civilians

Arab Front (Arab Liberation Front): political party within the PLO affiliated with the Iraqi regime

Armed Struggle (al-Kifah al-Musallah): security arm of the PLO responsible for coordinating military action

Dany Chamoun: Lebanese right-wing politician assassinated in 1990 by rival Lebanese factions

dabkeh: traditional folk dance of Palestine, as well as of Lebanon, Syria, and other parts of the Levant

Deuxième Bureau: a division of Lebanese military intelligence, which played an important role in surveillance and repression of Palestinian refugees in the 1950s and 1960s

Fairuz: prominent Lebanese singer (1934–), famous among Palestinians for having sung a number of songs for and about Jerusalem and Palestine

Fateh (Fatah): main political party within the PLO, established in 1959 and led until his death by Yasir 'Arafat

fida'i (pl. *fida'iyin*; *fedayeen*): literally, self-sacrificer; a term often used for a member of the Palestinian resistance, usually an armed fighter.

ful (foul): savoury dish with fava beans in lemon and garlic, eaten in various parts of the Middle East

gundelia (Arabic: *'aqqub*): thistle-like plant native to the Middle East, used in Palestine in stews and other dishes

George Habash: founder and leader of the Popular Front for the Liberation of Palestine (PFLP), nicknamed "al-Hakim" ("wise one" or "physician"), trained as a medical doctor before joining the Palestinian resistance

Sa'd Haddad: Lebanese army officer who created a pro-Israeli militia (South Lebanon Army) that was active in the Israeli-occupied zone in southern Lebanon from 1979 to 2000

hajjeh (f.), *hajj* (m.): literally, someone who has performed the pilgrimage to Mecca; often used as a respectful epithet to address elders

hakawati: traditional storyteller in Palestine and other parts of the Middle East, often entertaining audiences in cafés or teahouses

Hanzala: character created by the Palestinian political cartoonist Naji al-'Ali, now a symbol of Palestinian steadfastness whose image is widely reproduced in Palestinian iconography

hattah: traditional Arab scarf consisting of a white or patterned cloth worn over the head and sometimes held in place by *'iqal*

'iqal: circle of cord or rope holding in place *hatta* or *kufiyah* headdress around the crown of the head

Walid Junblatt: Lebanese politician allied with the Palestinian resistance movement during the Lebanese civil war

ka'k: one of a variety of sweet or savory crusty breads or baked goods, often topped with sesame seeds, popular in Palestine, Lebanon, and other parts of the Middle East *kanafeh*: pastry made with semolina and cheese, often served at breakfast or as dessert, in Palestine, Lebanon, Syria, and other parts of the Levant

khalo: term of endearment used for a maternal uncle (*khal*)

kufiyah (*keffiyeh*): traditional Arab scarf, often in a red-and-white or black-and-white pattern, worn over the head or across the shoulders, often as a symbol of affiliation with Palestinian liberation movements

labneh: strained yogurt, often eaten with bread at breakfast in Palestine and other parts of the Levant

mukhtar: headman of a village or town

Nakba: literally, catastrophe; term designating the dispossession and displacement of the people of Palestine in 1948, and the establishment of the state of Israel

Naksa: literally, setback; term designating the defeat of Arab armies by Israel in the June 1967 war (aka. the "Six-Day War")

oud (*'ud*): musical instrument with strings, shaped like a lute, used in most parts of the Middle East and North Africa

People of the Cave: protagonists of a Qur'anic tale about a group of pious people who hid in a cave to evade their persecutors and awoke hundreds of years later thinking that they had slept for just one night (based on the tale of the Cave Sleepers of Ephesus)

Phalangists: right-wing Lebanese political party espousing a Lebanese nationalist ideology, also known as Kata'ib (Kataeb)

Popular Front for the Liberation of Palestine (PFLP): political party within the PLO espousing a Marxist-Leninist ideology

al-Sa'iqa: political party within the PLO affiliated with the Syrian regime

Shaykh Imam: a popular Egyptian folk singer and composer (1918–1995), remembered for his radical leftist songs championing the poor and satirizing the Egyptian political class

sitti: term of endearment for a grandmother

suhur: predawn meal during the month of Ramadan, a time of fasting from sunrise to sundown

teta: term of endearment for a grandmother

thawb (*thobe*): Palestinian gown often embroidered with traditional patterns and worn on special occasions

Umm Kulthum: renowned Egyptian singer and songwriter (1904–1975), widely popular all over the Arab world

UNRWA (United Nations Relief and Works Agency): UN agency established in 1949 to provide relief to Palestinian refugees, which continues to provide rations, education, and other services in the refugee camps